WHO STOLE
*Sunday
Morning?*

Bishop Sir Walter Mack, Jr

WHO STOLE
Sunday Morning?

ACK
PUBLISHING

Who Stole Sunday Morning?
ISBN: 978-1-949106-34-3
Copyright © 2020 Dr. Sir Walter L.Mack Jr.

Published by Smack Publishing
1200 N. Trade Street
Winston-Salem, NC 27101

Produced and Distributed by
Word and Spirit Publishers
P.O. Box 701403
Tulsa, OK 74170
wordandspiritpublishing.com

DEDICATION

I would like to dedicate this book to my mother, Mrs. Frances Jones Mack, and my father, the late Dr. Sir Walter Mack, Sr. I am so thankful that both of them made Sunday Morning have meaning for me. I am today, because they refused to let anything steal our Sunday Morning.

I would also like to remember the late Mrs. Erma Bush, who had a profound love for dressing in hats on Sunday Mornings. We miss you! There is also a chapter in this book dedicated to all of those who have succumbed to the Coronavirus. We are praying for their families.

Lastly, this book is dedicated to my tremendous staff and volunteers of Union Baptist Church, and all they do to make Sunday Mornings have meaning in a time that is so critical. Blessings upon you, and thank you for your excellence.

SIR WALTER MACK

creative systems + implementation coach

BISHOP MACK'S SPECIAL NOTE TO YOU

CHAPTERS

This chapter will look at how people take the church for granted and how it affects the overall life of the church. Entitlement plays out in so many ways, and this chapter will inform you on how to know when a church is entitled.

This chapter addresses the self-esteem of the church, and how in many ways the church projects self hate. Read this chapter and discover the characteristics of low self-esteem, and how we can improve the self-image of the church.

Everything deserves an upgrade and a process of improvement. The church is no different. Read this chapter and discover the difference between traditions and traditionalism and what the church can do to remain relevant?

Many people are not in church today because church members are in stores and shopping malls. Read this chapter on what we can do to counter the temptation to shop rather than worship on Sunday Morning.

What will make a parent take his or her child out of Sunday School, and put his son or daughter on a basketball court on Sunday Morning? Read this chapter to discover the real plan of destruction behind AAU, and the strategy for churches to address it?

The Body of Christ is losing youth and young adults at alarming numbers. Much of our loss rests upon how youth see the world, and how the older generations see the world. Read and discover the impact that this is having on the white and black church.

Preachers are not perfect, but today it appears that imperfection is front and center. Read this chapter and look at strategies for helping preachers get it together. This chapter is designed to edify and not destroy.

Social media has come into almost every area of our life. Now, it has invaded the church. This chapter is about how to manage social media in your ministry, and will require you to assess whether it is helpful or hurtful.

Dr. Bill J. Leonard

FOREWORD
By
William D. Watley, PhD

WHO STOLE SUNDAY MORNING?

When the culture sneezes, the church catches the flu. There was a time when the church determined the look and the lifestyle of western civilization. There was a time when the censure and condemnation of the church carried weight in the policies, politics, and practices, as well as the marketing, messages and mores of the business, political and educational communities of our society and culture. There was a time when the church was the center of life and scheduling for the American family in general, and the African American family in particular. "Back in the day" when I was growing up, when I asked other young people, "What church do you go to or attend?—the assumption was that everyone went or belonged to some brand-named church. One of the colloquialisms of that era was that "If a black person is not either Baptist, Methodist, or Holiness (Pentecostal), then somebody has been messing with their religion."

"Back in the day" when I was growing up, a number of us had three categories of clothes—church clothes, school clothes, and play clothes—and never the twain shall meet. "Back in the day" when I was growing up, Sunday was "the Lord's day." In the majority of households, going to church and doing church, were the central and sometimes only activities that were allowed in a number of households. Except for the most necessary activities, such as preparing Sunday Morning breakfast or dinner or supper, housework was forbidden. The economic enterprises and businesses, bowed to the God of Sunday and closed their doors for the most part. Restaurants were allowed to remain open so they could feed the Sunday worshippers who rushed to them and ate with as much passion and freedom as they had earlier expressed in worship.

Fast forward to today, when the voice of the Church in western culture has become muffled, smothered and some-times lost amidst the voices of a competing, conflicting, and abrasive political climate where self-serving political inter-ests abound. Fast forward to today, when money yells with gusto, and the teachings of the word of God are timidly and apologetically whispered. Fast forward to today, when the God of Sunday has been dethroned by a burgeoning business environment that is fed by an out of control consumerism and a populace which has adopted a "Judges 21: 25" mantra. This mentality asserts a profane and misguided individualism wherein every person, not a larger moral community, determine what is right and what is wrong for himself and herself. Fast forward to today in which many churches are struggling to stay in the soul saving business while the field for the harvest of souls is overflowing more than ever. Fast forward to today when Christianity and its historic voice, the "mainline" churches, are struggling to survive in a time of plenty.

Integral to the growth of the kingdom of God has been the regular and consistent gathering of the body of Christ called church on the Lord's Day (Sunday), at which time the faith was proclaimed and taught, and the saints were encouraged, edified, enlightened and then sent forth to engage the communities in which they lived with the Gospel of the Lord Jesus Christ. However, what happens when Sunday, the Lord's day has become a shopping day, a sporting events day, and a day of rest and leisure as defined by the particular tastes and desires of each individual?

In this book, Bishop Sir Walter Lee Mack, Jr., with passion, purpose as well as scholarly research and keen discernment and insight, addresses the dilemma and reality of the dethroning of Sunday Morning as the fulcrum for Christian nurture and kingdom witness and expansion. How does Sunday Morning regain its savor for both the majority of individuals who should be filling the pews, but are presently filling shopping malls and the bleachers at sporting events?

Many years ago, the Reverend Dr. Martin Luther King, Jr. asked the question, *"Where Do We Go From Here: Chaos Or Community?"* The contents and insights in this very much needed work by Bishop Mack will help provide answers to Dr. King's destiny question that we as a civilization, a nation, and the church of God, are still struggling to resolve.

MATTHEW 28:12-20 (NKJV)

When they had assembled with the elders and consulted together, they gave a large sum of money to the soldiers, **13** saying, "Tell them, 'His disciples came at night and stole Him away while we slept.' **14** And if this comes to the governor's ears, we will appease him and make you secure." **15** So they took the money and did as they were instructed; and this saying is commonly reported among the Jews until this day. **16** Then the eleven disciples went away into Galilee, to the mountain which Jesus had appointed for them. **17** When they saw Him, they worshiped Him; but some doubted. **18** And Jesus came and spoke to them, saying, "All authority has been given to Me in heaven and on earth. **19** Go therefore and make disciples of all the nations, baptizing them in the name of the Father and of the Son and of the Holy Spirit, **20** teaching them to observe all things that I have commanded you; and lo, I am with you always, even to the end of the age." Amen.

The Plot

*T*his relevant question of "Who Stole Sunday Morning?" is not a new question, but the pondering of the matter is actually biblical and has a two-thousand-year track record. The premise for this thought is biblically established in Matthew 28, when the resurrection of Jesus had taken place. The phenomenon of the resurrection was such that Jesus, before dying declared that He would rise. While we know today in our hearts that He did get up from the dead, there were many who still didn't believe that Jesus was God Incarnate, and that His purpose was to die for the sins of the world, and resurrect in three days with all power in His hands. So when the resurrection happened, the word was spread abroad by the women who were at the tomb, the guards who heard of what occurred, and eventually the disciples who told others, "Jesus is alive."

The Tension

Now in the midst of this life announcement, a conspiracy is devised, and the conspiracy was simply this: When the guards went to tell the high priest what had taken place in the garden of the tomb, the guards were encouraged to circulate a lie. Here is the lie they were instructed to tell: Don't tell the world that Jesus rose from the grave, but rather say that in the night someone came and stole the body while we were sleeping. The soldiers took the bribe and did as they were told. That story cooked up in the Jewish High Council, is still going around in some places today (Matthew 28:15 MSG).

This very obvious misleading of the truth establishes the idea that the conspiracy to "steal the body of Jesus" was necessary to be told, if the attempt to reduce the value and power of Jesus' authority would be minimized. In other words, this was the first attempt to reduce Christianity to a mere fallacy, fake news, or worse a lie played out on humanity. Who stole Sunday Morning, started with this fallacy, because essentially Jesus is "Sunday Morning." He is the very reason for "Sunday Morning." He is the reason that Sunday even has significance.

The Reality

Therefore, this book is written to simply say, that the conspiracy that was established in the Bible that His body was stolen, has in many respects become a reality today. In many ways there seems to be evidence that somebody has stolen "Sunday Morning," putting at risk the existence of the body of Christ. When the church is missing, the body of Christ is missing. That is His body. What this writing is intended to do is address the decline of church participation, while looking at some things we can do to stop the enemy from stealing "Sunday Morning."

While I am well aware that we are living in an age where church does not just happen on "Sunday Morning," throughout this book, "Sunday Morning" will be used as a marking for anytime or any day that we have worship, and it does not change the fact that there is an enemy who is out to kill, steal, and destroy His body— The Church of the Living God.

A Survey of Sunday Morning

My book, *Creative Ministry Moves,* was prompted by the need to address the steady decline of "church members" actually going to church. I would like to borrow a portion of that writing to express that idea of a stolen Sunday Morning.

The Church is leaving the church.

All research data, and the diminishing numbers we see as pastors and church leaders will clearly reflect there is something going on today, when "the Church" is now leaving the church. I'm not speaking of leaving in regards to evangelism, or leaving the church to witness, but it is becoming more apparent that the Church is not even going to church. There are many churches doing quite well with attendance, and may not have a problem with the "empty pew" Sunday. Before you celebrate, it is important that you remember your church is not "the Church." You are a branch on the tree. But if we were to do an examination of the tree at its root, you would have to confess that bark is falling off of the tree; decay has set in, and the tree appears to be dying.

The Church is leaving the church. This is a concern that is spreading throughout the nation, and has many pastors and church leaders raising questions and asking, "Where are the church members this Sunday Morning?"

The best way I can describe this experience is in the following memoir. One Sunday while driving to church along my regular route, I saw cars taking an alternate route. I wasn't quite sure what was taking place ahead of me, but when I approached closer I discovered there was a detour sign directing us another way. When I followed the detour sign, shortly thereafter, I noticed the detour sign was there because there was a marathon race taking place on Sunday Morning. There were hundreds of people in the race on Sunday Morning at a time when traditionally people would be in church. It occurred to me that there is a detour sign set up to direct people from the church today, and just as the marathon is taking place, there are many people today who are latterly running away from the church. Regardless of what city you live in, just leave the church one Sunday Morning at the time of worship and drive past the nearest Wal-Mart, Home Depot, Lowes, Starbucks, AAU Basketball Court, or youth dance club auditorium and don't be surprised if you find people who were once in church now replacing church with an activity that has nothing to do with God.

There is a crisis taking place today in the church, and it appears as if " the Church" is leaving the church. What is happening today is that people don't value church. They feel as if they don't need the church, and in some way, haven't even thought about the church. Consider these striking statistics as we prepare to engage the idea of creative evangelism.

- 83% of Americans are not attending a conventional church on the weekend. This idea is supported by *The Journal for the Scientific Study of Religion* by sociologists C. Kirk Hadaway and Penny Long Marler—known for their scholarly research on the church. Their findings reveal that the actual rate of church attendance from head counts is less than half of the 40 percent the pollsters report. Numbers from actual counts of people in Orthodox Christian churches (Catholic, mainline and evangelical) show that in 2004, 17.7 percent of the population attended a Christian church on any given weekend. 52 million people were reported instead of the pollster-reported 132 million (40 percent).

- 85% of all churches in North America have reached a plateau where no growth is happening, and the growth that is happening is coming from what they know as switchers. "Switchers" are people who leave one church and simply join another church.

This does not dictate Christian growth, as much as it does individual church growth.

- Every year, approximately 4000 new churches open their doors. Every year approximately 7000 churches close their doors for the last time.

- Only 28% of younger Americans between 23 and 37 attend church. Other generations range between 43% and 52%. This is a significant drop in generational attendance and a large reason why many churches are seeing a decline in attendance.

- 59% of Millennials who grew up in churches are leaving.

One particular denomination did a survey on its leadership ministries. The results are as follows:

- 63% of the leadership in this denomination, including deacons and elders, have not led one stranger to Jesus in the last two years through the method of "Go Ye" evangelism.

- 49% of the leadership ministries spend zero time in an average week ministering outside of the church.

- 89% of the leadership ministries have zero time reserved on their list of weekly priorities for going out to evangelize. *Street Level Evangelism* by

Michael Parrott, *Acts Evangelism,* Spokane, WA, 1993, pp. 9-11.

A survey was done from select pastors in the United States, and the question was raised. Have you seen a decline in your worship attendance, and how has it impacted your church?

- "There has been a global decline in church attendance in the last five years, and many pastors are becoming depressed because their numbers are smaller." –**Bishop Neil C. Ellis, Mt. Tabor Union Baptist in Nassau, Bahamas.**

Christian Post- Sunday, July 7, 2019.

- "I have noticed a decline in worship, and it seems that people pick and choose which Sunday they will come. It has impacted our church financially and we no longer can provide ministry at the level we are accustomed because of the decline in our income as well." –**Bishop Sir Walter Mack, Union Baptist Church, Winston-Salem, North Carolina**

- "I have seen a decline and have been criticized for it. While our attendance is in decline, our giving is up. I have closed off the balcony until downstairs is 90 percent full." –**Dr. Robert Charles Scott, St. Paul Baptist Church, Charlotte, North Carolina.**

- "We have seen a decline in physical attendance across all three of our campuses, and at the same time, an exponential rise in the number of people that chose to worship via the internet. The residual effect of the physical decline is fewer services, and conversely a greater investment in constructing digital communities and exploring that space for the benefit of the kingdom." –**Dr. Lance Watson, St. Paul Baptist Church, Richmond, Virginia.**

- "The decline has not only hurt the church financially, it has hurt the church spiritually. When we separate, we lose human sensitivity that results in a failure to hear, see and feel the pains of the flesh-church. In essence, we draw strength from each other. Also, the Christian witness begins losing credibility. We preach and impress the nothingness of humanity without God. Yet, it appears that people are separating themselves from worship and are still seemingly doing well. This plants the mindset that people are their own sustaining source. We know this to be false; however, it still becomes a force that the church has to constantly contend with." –**Reverend Kathy Dunton, St. Peters United Methodist Church, Oxford, North Carolina**

- "The decline in attendance seen at The Freedom Church of Gwinnett has amounted to less ministry engagement. Whereas people generally attended 3 to 4 times a month. They now visit 1 to 2 times a month. Volunteers are now prioritizing secular events over spiritual impact and serving opportunities. My search has involved reconnecting with our identity through the Afrocentric pulse of Christianity. We must remember who we are!" –**Dr. Gregory Baker, Freedom Church, Atlanta, Georgia.**

This book is written to address this issue of church decline. While we will consider reasons for this decline in church attendance, more importantly, it is my intent to look at ways we can stop the bleeding. What is it that we can do to curtail this decline of church attendance? Who and what is behind the decline of church attendance? What are some things we can do to deter the thief that is coming to steal Sunday Morning?

SPECIAL DEDICATED CHAPTER TO ALL WHO PASSED FROM THE CORONAVIRUS

A Virus Stole Sunday Morning

*D*uring the time of this writing the Coronavirus has hit the globe. A vicious virus that that lends to the reality that death may follow. The name "corona" is derived from the Latin word, meaning "crown or halo". When this disease hit our globe, China, Europe, and United States in particular, sickness and death was the result for many like never seen in this modern time before. However, when I saw the words "crown" and "halo", this took it to a biblical place for me.

While some scientist traced this virus to a bat in China, this does not negate for me that "Crown" and "halo" are biblical terms which established for me a divine plan during this plague. Plagues are biblical, and if the Bible was still been written, this plague would have been in it. While I know there are many who feel that God has absolutely nothing to do with this virus, there are times when God will hurtfully impart His judgement, not to mention, using a plague to do so. Plagues are biblical, and God often used plagues to get the attention of wicked Kings, and people who participated in the wicked King's rule. Because the Old Testament is induced with "corporate personality" meaning whatever happened to one, happened to all, many innocent people will suffer and become victim to this plague. From a biblical perspective, when plagues broke out in the land, people could not function as normal, people lived in fear, fields couldn't be harvested. Isaiah 26:20, declared, Go, my people, enter your rooms and shut the doors behind you; hide yourselves for a little while until his wrath has passed by. In Exodus 12:7, Then they are to take some of **the** blood and put it on the sides and tops of the doorframes of the houses where they eat the lambs. This was so that when the death angel would pass, it would be deterred to touch the home where the blood of the lamb was sacrificed.

Due to the severity of the virus hitting our land, fear, little access, and even quarantine was necessary. Believe it or not, this virus led to the cancelation of schools, work assignments, sporting events, and even stole Sunday Morning worship services at local churches. For the first time in my lifetime, church buildings were closed for

Easter. When the virus hit, churches had to cancel meetings, events, and even worship. Since this virus was announced as a transmutable disease, many preachers led this effort to be very cautious with the gathering of people in one setting. This virus gave impetus for the Center of Disease Control had to declare a national emergency, and gatherings no larger than 10 to gather at one time. This virus was set to take the lives of more than 200,000 people in the span of a few months. Because of this, many churches had to cancel worship, not to mention entire cities being quarantined.

There are many beliefs about where the virus originated. However, while the origin may never be one hundred percent identified, what we do know is that God is Sovereign, and God can use anything for the purpose of Kingdom impact. What is God saying through a virus like this? What possibly could be the intent of God permitting such a virus on human creation. While we know that sickness, disease, and viruses does not emulate from God, God can use these things to get the attention of humanity back to Himself. Could it be that through this virus, God is trying to get us to see His crown again or should I say Sunday morning again? Plagues in the Bible happened primarily for two reasons; first to show the adversary that God was all powerful. Secondly, to show the people of God, that no idol god would ever take His place. So, it is with the culture for which we live today. We have put many things before God. We have allowed sports to replace the time we spend in on Sunday morning. Considering that more fans pack stadiums, than they do pews. However, the virus made it such that fans couldn't even attend games. We have put our work and employment before the sanctity of God, but the virus made it such that jobs shut down, and layoffs took place. We have put cruises, flights, and vacations before God, but when the virus hit, many were too scared to take trips. Many took church for granted, and made church something to do out of routine, and not a place to worship God in spirit and in truth. Where is God in all of this? God is just using a virus to get us back where He wants us to be. Isolated, set aside, and quarantined for His glory. How is God getting glory from this virus? Consider the good side of a bad virus.

The Good Side of a Bad Virus

THIS VIRUS HAS CAUSED US TO RESET

1. This virus has called the world to a place of reset. A time of quarantine allows people to reset their priorities, relationships, finances, employment and even their worship. In my opinion, God has shut the world down. I wonder if after the cure comes, will we go back to packing out stadiums, while our church pews are

empty? Will we go back to charging ridiculous prices, like $8 for a mask that cost 89 cents? Will we go back to funding a wall, when our children should have had computers for their homes all the time? Will gangs start shooting again, because since the virus I have not heard of one shooting in our city?

THIS VIRUS HAS MOVED US TO CREATIVITY

2. This virus has awakened the giant of creativity. I am so inspired to see churches who in the past fought and rejected change, transition, technology, and simply another way of doing things, now being forced to come out of the box and do things another way. Tradition is living faith of the dead. Traditionalism is the dead faith of the living. God just destroyed traditionalism in some churches.

THIS VIRUS HAS REVEALED THAT GOD IS NOT DEAD

3. This virus has revealed that God is not dead. Do you really think that God was going to let our nation get away with putting babies in cages, calling nations' S-hole countries, tolerate the lack of integrity and Christian behavior in high places? Do you think that we would not have to pay for many Christian endorsing and embracing behavior politically that is so far removed

from who God is? I was appalled when President Trump referred to himself as Savior, and don't forget the time he stated that he alone "was about to make God look better"? God is not dead. No Republican, Democrat, or Independent should refer to themselves as a "Savior" or even suggest that they have done more for Christianity than Jesus has done, these were words quoted by the President in a recent news article.

THIS VIRUS HAS SHOWN THERE ARE SOME GOOD PEOPLE IN THE WORLD

4. This virus has revealed that our nation is not as torn as we thought. There are some good white people, black people, and brown people that really care. We are all having to depend on one another right now. The virus does not recognize skin color.

THIS VIRUS HAS REVEALED OUR ABILITY

5. This virus has revealed that what we are doing now, could have been done all the time.

  - The virus revealed that America could afford laptops for every child in school

  - The virus revealed that buildings in our communities could be used for homeless shelters

- The virus revealed that pregnant women, disabled people & single parents could've worked from home the entire time.

  This virus has revealed that bill payments, evictions notices, co-pays, and other out-of-pocket health provider fees could have been waived the entire time.

- This virus has revealed that airfare could've been cheaper this whole time.

The bottom line is that there is a good side to this virus, however, we are praying for safety and sustained life for those who may be infected.

If we are going get people back in church, it begins by getting people back in the presence of God personally first. A plague or a virus will make people want God differently, desire to go deeper with Him, if nothing else, they want God to save them. Wow, this is amazing that "mass deliverance" could be the result of a virus. While this is not the first virus that sought to get God's people out of the presence of God. There is a virus called "sin" that had the original intent of not just stealing Sunday morning, but "sin" is also after our soul. When this virus entered, God gave us an Anti-Vaccine called Jesus Christ. Christ built up our immune system with faith to stand against the illness that comes with the virus of original sin. Though we are born in sin, and shaped in iniquity, what helps us to maintain, is when we make our way to the hospital called the church. When the Coronavirus hit the globe, even people that didn't go to church, now wanted to come to church. The church is the hospital, that offers to the world a balm called blood, that by faith is good for the healing from sin.

The Dedication

To all who have succumbed to this very vicious virus, we remember you in a very special way. Your loss is not in vain, people are coming back to church.

Please List the Names of Those You Know Who Lost Their Lives to The Coronavirus

_____

_____

_____

_____

_____

_____

_____

1

SPOILED, ENTITLED SAINTS

Stole Sunday Morning

But he giveth more grace. Wherefore he saith, God resisteth the proud, but giveth grace unto the humble. –**James 4:6**

*I*t was in 1974 when a call came to our home shortly after midnight, that our church, the Emmanuel Baptist Church of Winston-Salem was in flames. My father serving as the pastor, rushed from the home while we followed, and arrived there to see that the church was on fire. For the next two years the church would have to meet in recreational centers, funeral homes, and churches that had space to offer, while bearing the challenge of keeping its members together. While the physical church burned to the ground, the 'ecclesia" the body of Christ stayed together and remained strong.

Regardless of where we were having church for that week, the church was packed, and attendance was never a concern or worry. We were strong! There was no sense of anyone in worship taking worship for granted. Every Sunday was "packed," and it was this feeling of being together, that gave us the assurance that while the building may have burned down, "the Church" — the people of God — were standing strong. It was this urgency of remaining strong in spite of loss, that the church refused to embrace, adopt, or even be open to the spirit of entitlement. Even though loss was so immanent, throughout the entire congregation church members felt that people were still blessed, thankful, and appreciative for what God had done in their past.

In many places today, this is not the case. Within the American Protestant and Catholic church, there seems to be an entitlement that has set into the body of Christ, where many today approach the church from the perspective of being an "option" and not a "necessity." Years ago church was indeed the highlight and the primary focus of the week. Attending church was the thing to do, and it was all too popular it seemed among every culture and community. People went to church, and when they attended, they were "dressed to kill," meaning they had on their Sunday best. They came looking like a million dollars before taxes, when in fact, many of those Saints probably didn't have a dime in their pocket.

Growing up in the 70's and 80's, it seemed that everybody I knew was a member of a church somewhere. Preachers then were very intentional about preparing a message with the canvas of the mind and heart as their primary objective. Choirs would wear robes, and how could we forget in the African American church tradition, Sunday afternoon anniversaries, where the choirs marched in to showcase their new music in their new robes. "I remember sitting there in my father's rural community church, Buncombe Baptist Church in Lexington, North Carolina, with elbows hitting me in the face because every pew held breathing room only." We could smell the aroma of the chicken being cooked from downstairs coming through the air vents, and there was great anticipation that after we were fed spiritually, we were going to be fed physically. On Sundays, people were in church. Church was family; church was a conduit to community. Church was the epicenter of all that would take place for the improvement of lifestyle. In some settings you could actually hear the worship before you arrived to worship. Participation was strong, auxiliaries were active, pulpits were well occupied with preachers who took preaching seriously, and the members supported without much strain and begging.

However today, there is a flip in how we understand church. In the past the church was passed down from one generation to the next. Today with there being a decrease in millennial participation, it seems that the church is missing the next group to pass the baton to. This is very difficult for us to conceive because in our minds, the church will always be here. This is the "entitlement factor" which we are facing today, and the entitlement presence is taking up pews everywhere regardless of church size, denomination, racial makeup, or region of location. Consider the few ways in which entitlement has stolen Sunday Morning. So many believe they deserve privileges.

Entitlement Robs Attendance

Tullian Tchividjian expounded on entitlement is such a profound way, when he stated, "legalism breeds us into sense of entitlement, that turns us into complainers."

Entitlement for the church plays out in a way that we are ministering in a culture, that really only sees the church as necessary upon need. When we don't need the church, then its relevance is reduced to the lowest common denominator. Think of the "baddest" child you know. This is the child who does not say, "Excuse me," "Please," "Thank you," or "I'm sorry." This picture of an "entitled child" should also help you to understand the personality profile of "entitled" people in the church. "Entitled people" show little concern for the church's history, vision, responsibilities, obligations or the ministries that she has in place. When the church expresses itself in a way that shows lack of support, attendance, and care for Christ and community, you can easily sense the presence of an entitled spirit.

When the church expresses itself in a way that shows lack of support, attendance, and care for Christ and community, you can easily sense the presence of an entitled spirit.

Whatever happened to the time when church attendance was put on the psychological and soul agenda, bearing invisible ink that could not be seen with the naked eye? However, the "entitlement factor" has people only responding to the church if they agree with the theology of the church, or if the church has something that interests them, or if they can simply get what they want out of it. Eugene Peterson in his book, *The Unnecessary Pastor,* gives hint to this idea that as a pastor, your presence and place is really unnecessary until there is an emergency or a need. You are not needed for just "being," you are needed for "doing." This faulty theology and sick sociology has inundated the church today, and it is coming out in bazar actions and requests.

Recently, I was asked to do a funeral of an individual who had not been to our church in 20 years or more. I was told that the deceased was a member under the former pastor, and the family desired for the ministry to honor that membership as active. Needless to say, I had to inform them that because of the deceased's lack of support to the ministry, we could not classify the person as a member of the church, but would be glad to assist them in their time of need. Nevertheless, what was so interesting to me, is that no one apologized about the lack of their support over the course of twenty-years, and they really did expect the church to just pick up the pieces and act like twenty years missing was not a problem. To add impact to injury, those who were active in the ministry who knew the deceased, began giving me the cold shoulder because such a position was taken. Entitlement in attendance makes you think, "There is no need to support the church whenever I can, because the church owes me something, and it should exist to satisfy me and what I desire." Here is what goes through the mind of an entitled person when they want to have their way. "If I want it, it's mine. If I give it to you, and change my mind later, it's mine. If I can take it away from you, it's mine. If I had it a little while ago, it's mine. If we are building something together, it's mine. If it looks just like mine, it's mine." "Entitled Saints" think the very same way; in their minds, "there is nothing else we need to do to enhance the church, grow the church, develop the church, because whatever the church is or is not, 'it is mine.'" So why attend, when it already belongs to me? Why support when it will always be there? Why share in its responsibilities, when there is always somebody that will do their part and my part? This is the spirit of entitlement, and it is affecting what happens on Sunday Morning.

Entitlement Hinders Participation

Because entitlement has us believing that the church will always be in place, it makes sense that there is no real urgency for some to support the mission and vision of the church. There was a time in ministry where you didn't have to beg people to testify, sing, serve, work, or financially support the ministry in any capacity. However, today there seems to be a lack of participation and it is not a guarantee that there will be someone in place to even handle some of the most valuable parts of the ministry. Entitlement has the body of Christ believing "if I don't do it, somebody else will get it done." While it is true that others can make things happen in the ministry, it still does not negate your doing your part. I believe that when God sends people to ministries, that there is an intentional purpose for that gift to be used in that local assembly. While others may be able to perform your duty, the real reward comes when you use your gift for the purpose it was established. Justin Buzzard declared, "it is grace that destroys entitlement."

It takes each person doing his or her part to support the ministry spiritually, physically, and financially. Entitlement that lends itself to non-participation, non-involvement, and non-support, could also be interpreted that members are not thankful, and really don't appreciate all that God has done. Therefore, the lack of participation is really a way of saying, "God you were supposed to do what you did for me, and I don't owe you anything for it. That's a picture of entitlement at its best.

Entitlement Affects Giving

Recently we conducted a stewardship analysis in our congregation, and discovered that our ministry was underperforming financially, that there were many members who had not been giving as they should. There is a direct link to the lack of enthusiasm for attendance, participation and giving. Entitlement brings one to a place where the precepts and mandates given by God will make us feel as if those things do not apply to us. However, as it pertains to supporting the church financially, God's tithing paradigm, God's giving requirements, and God's expectation for the church to have generosity should be a lifestyle for all. We have been taught Matthew 6:21. **21** "For where your trea-sure is, there your heart will be also." Many people mis-quote this scripture and say, "Where your heart is that is where your treasure is also. However, that is not what this scripture says. It says, where your treasure is, that is where your heart is. In other words, the heart follows the invest-ment, and not the investment the heart. There are some things that I have in my home that I value very much, because I know the money that I have invested to have it. The investment makes the difference in the value. My heart follows my treasure.

If you want to know where people are in their heart, just consider where they spend their money. More often than not, many are not convinced that most of their money should be in the church, because they are not in church. But when Sunday Morning becomes your lifestyle, your investment will soon be followed by your heart. This explains why in the introduction of this book that some pastors said they experienced physical decline, but finan-cial increase. It is because there are those who have the ministry so deep in their hearts, that even when they can't get there physically, they still support financially. Which says something about their heart. "Where your treasure is, your heart is also."

Lets Talk About Sunday Morning-
How Do We Correct The Spirit of Entitlement?

Don't Let Entitlement Steal Sunday Morning

This sense of entitlement has the potential of eradicating "the Church" and aborting its purpose. If the church does not support "the Church," then "the Church" will soon fade away and die. While it is important that we support the church physically, emotionally, and spiritually, it is also important that we give financially towards its mission and function, or the church will be stolen. If the church members do not support the church, bills can't be paid; salaries can't be supported, missions can't be financed, excellence can't be executed, insurances can't be paid; and the church can't sustain itself financially to do ministry. Do not assume that everybody in church is supporting the church financially; therefore, it takes everyone doing their part and making money in the ministry a priority.

If we are going to address the issue of Who Stole Sunday Morning, it is imperative that the church members pray and vehemently work against the spirit of entitlement. Entitlement works from the idea that nothing is urgent for me to do, because there will always be others who will do it. While this is true to some degree, the other side to this is everyone must do his or her part, and don't wait for the next person to do it. Your regular attendance, participation and giving, are signs that you appreciate God in such a way, that whatever God needs from you, you are willing to follow. When Sunday Morning comes, make it your priority to physically be in church if you are physically able, and if not, online worship service should be your last resort, but let nothing hinder you from a Sunday Morning with God and the Saints.

Hebrews 10:23-25 reminds you, "Let us hold fast the profession of our faith without wavering . . . Not forsaking the assembling of ourselves together, as the manner of some is, but exhorting one another: and so much the more as you see the day approaching."

Group Discussion Questions For Sunday Morning

1. Why do you think people feel entitled today?

   _____

   _____

   _____

2. What are some things you have to change about yourself, not to appear as if you are entitled?

   _____

   _____

   _____

3. What are you going to do to enhance your worship attendance?_____

_____

_____

4. What are some things that you have to change from your schedule to participate more in church?

_____

_____

_____

5. How are you going to support the church better financially?

_____

_____

_____

2

LOW CHURCH SELF-ESTEEM

Stole Sunday Morning

"I praise you because I am fearfully and wonderfully made; your works are wonderful, I know that full well." –**Psalm 139:14 (NIV)**

*I*t's a problem when you don't like yourself. It's hard to get people to think you are beautiful, when you think of yourself as ugly. It's hard to attract the right people in your destiny, when the portrayal of yourself is negative, without energy, and lacking confidence. It's not what we are that often keeps us from being all that we are, it is what we perceive ourselves not to be. So is the image of a church with low self-esteem. Who wants to come to a church that hates itself? Who wants to join a church that even the members hate attending? Who wants to support a church where nothing is ever right, where nothing can ever be satisfactory, where nothing positive can ever be spoken of? This is the image of a church with low self-esteem.

Low self-esteem works from the perspective that what God intended us to be, we believe ourselves to be not.

One of the most vital components that stole Sunday Morning is low Church self-esteem. Low self-esteem works from the perspective that what God intended us to be, we believe ourselves to be not. Maxwell Maltz said that "low self-esteem is like driving through life with your hand-brake on." There was a time when the church actually believed in the church; however, today it seems as if the brakes are on the church, and our belief seems to have been compromised.

In order for us to understand the esteem of the early church, it is important that we do a firm evaluation of what exactly established the belief system of the early church. Acts 2:1-4 says, "And when the day of Pentecost was fully come, they were all sitting with one accord in one place, and suddenly, there came a sound from heaven, as of a rushing mighty wind . . . it filled the house where they were sitting, and they were all filled with the Holy Ghost. . ."

Teaching Builds Self-Esteem

I am very confident in how I wear my suits and coordinate them with my neck-ties because at a very young age I learned this practice from my father. By example, he taught me the proper way a man should wear certain accessories with clothing, therefore, I wear them with confidence and much esteem.

In the book of Acts, it is very apparent that the self-esteem of the church has its foundation from the teaching of the Apostles. It is more than likely that what the Apostles were teaching was indeed what we call the Apostles' Creed: The Doctrine of the Father, the Son, and the Holy Spirit. In other words, the Church's esteem came from the idea that if they were going to possess power and authority, they had to be taught the Word of God, the thoughts of God, the belief system of God, by the sent messenger of God. It is apparent to me, that the self-esteem of the church has been impacted because we have veered away from our belief system, because we don't know what it is that we believe. If "the Church's" esteem is going to be restored, it is going to be important that the church leaders, the pastor in particular, fall in love with teaching doctrine all over again. Who is God the Father, God the Son, God the Holy Spirit? This is not to say that others can't help teach doctrine, but there is a hope that is established with the pastor, the leader, who takes time to elevate the esteem of the people with imparting vision and projection of ministry, while giving clarity about God and His role in our life. Our esteem starts there. We are wonderfully and beautifully made in the image of God according to Psalms 139:14-15. "I will praise you; for I am fearfully and wonderfully made: marvelous are your works; and that my soul knows right well." Consider these profound thoughts that will help shape the esteem of the church.

- "It is never too late to be what you might have been." –**George Eliot**

- "The best day of your life is the one on which you decide your life is your own. No apologies or excuses. No one to lean on, rely on, or blame. The gift is yours – it is an amazing journey – and you alone are responsible for the quality of it. This is the day your life really begins." –**Bob Moawad**

- "Too many people overvalue what they are not and undervalue what they are." –**Malcolm S. Forbes**

- "Never be bullied into silence. Never allow yourself to be made a victim. Accept no one's definition of your life, but define yourself." –**Harvey Fierstein**

Fellowship Can Fix Low Self - Esteem

In the book of Acts, after they received the Holy Spirit, the early Christians fellowship; they connected, and they actually enjoyed being with one another. In this age of technology, of which we will discuss in a later chapter, we have to be very careful that we do not allow live streaming worship and technological communication to destroy our real need for "koinonia" or fellowship. So the relevant question is, "How are we allowing the lack of fellowship to steal Sunday Morning kindling of spirit?" In this modern age of teaching right intelligence about giving, are we teaching that tithing is God's plan for financing the kingdom? Many churches have completely gone away from fish fry's and chicken dinner sales on Saturday morning for fundraising. I am about to suggest something radical, and that is I am about to suggest that we return back to fish fry's and chicken dinners cooked in the church kitchen, not so much for the money, but for the fellowship. This ties into the next point, that the early church went from house to house, breaking bread and eating together, I will unpack that next.

If Sunday Morning is going to take on life again, it is important that we work on our self-esteem by enjoying each other again. The church must like "the Church." This means we must guard each other's reputations on social media, we must protect pastors and church people who fall, and not exploit their fallen state before unbelievers. We must not compete with one another, and earnestly pray for each of us to win. The church must build up the church and edify the esteem of the church through real fellowship and spending time with one another.

Breaking Bread Can Heal Low Self-Esteem

There are three places in the New Testament where we see bread broken. The first place is when Jesus is in the Upper Room before His crucifixion, and He breaks bread before His disciples and declares that His body shall also be broken. The second time is after His resurrection, when He goes to the home of the disciples on the Emmaus Road, and He breaks bread and their eyes are opened. The third time of breaking bread is after the church receives the power of the Holy Spirit. Each time the bread is broken, it is for the purpose of reminding the followers and " the Church" that you cannot be a follower of Christ or a disciple in the church and not get broken.

You will be amazed to know the number of people who have low-self esteem about their Christianity because they believed that it is embarrassing to be a Christian while at the same time facing some most embarrassing situations. As a matter of fact, there is a theology that has directly impacted the theology of the church by teaching that Christians should not have to suffer, get sick, have problems, and even face tragedy or trials. Nothing could be further from the truth. Who gave these false theologians the right to take the blood of Jesus and turn it into kool-aid? We will have trials and tribulations, but Jesus says, "Be of good cheer, for I have overcome the world" (John 16:33).

It is interesting that at this meal, the early church was sure to have rice, grain, flour, oil, and leaven. The rice, grain, and flour represented the traditional meal, but the oil represented the work of Christ, and the leaven represented the sin of the Church. In other words, while the Church has the presence of sin in it, the power of Christ is still working. If this does not help the self-esteem of " the Church," I don't know what will. We can feel good about the fact that even though we fall, even though we make mistakes, Christ is still working on our behalf.

Let's Talk Sunday Morning—
How Do We Correct Low Self - Esteem?

Holiness, Miracles, and Revelation Handles
Low Self-Esteem

The church has no reason to have low self-esteem. The early church established for us to live and embrace holiness as a lifestyle. Holiness has very little to do with a denomination, but holiness is realizing that when you have been chosen by God, you have a purpose. Holiness means being comfortable with being separated from the world, and uniquely portrayed as God's chosen people. Holiness is "the Church's" circumcision from the world, for the purpose of holistic image and fulfillment. If "the Church" would return back to its identity of being the leader and not the follower, Christians will find esteem all over again. The LORD will make you the head, not the tail. If you pay attention to the commands of the LORD your God that I give you this day and carefully follow them, you will always be at the top, never at the bottom (Deuteronomy 28:13).

We are the head, and not the tail, above, and not beneath.

This is why we must remind worshippers that there is even an obligation in how we show up to worship. While I am all for relaxed dress codes in worship today to accommodate people particularly during intensely heated days, some of what we see enter into the church today as dress code does by no means represent holiness. Ladies, it is not appropriate to wear clothing that exposes your most intimate body parts in worship, or clothing that is so tight we see your defined body features such as cleavage before we see your God countenance. Let me put it this way, when considering what to wear to worship, it must be more than a beach towel, and you can't fit New York in a jump suit.

Gentlemen, no doubt "muscles" are sexy, and tight, sexy shirts for worship may not be the best presentation for God, because we ultimately want people to know of His strength and not see your muscles. Now if you are buffed there is only so much hiding of your muscles you can do, but God knows your heart, and your intent makes all the difference in terms of how you approach holiness. While relaxed dress codes are popular for you today as well, holiness is not best represented with your pants down below your waist, and uncared for grooming does not necessarily speak to the excellence which God calls us. A Principal of a High School in Winston-Salem, posts signs on every hall that says, "Show Us Your Mind, Not Your Behind." While I am clear that the God in us has very little to do with how we look on the outside, I am also clear that it's hard to talk to someone about God who will clothe you, and you have no shirt on your back. In short, we must be an example for the world, while being separate from the world.

Let's remind our children that it is acceptable if they don't dress like other children, or don't curse in their rap songs like other youth. Let's instruct our young ladies and our young men to always carry themselves and embrace being uniquely who they are. Holiness means chosen by God to represent God. According to Romans 12:2, "Be not conformed to this world; But be ye transformed by the renewing of your mind."

Revelation

Revelation is that which does not necessarily see what is, but sees things as they should be. One of the reasons that "the Church" has lost its self-esteem is because we no longer value revelation, hence, seeing that which we don't see. We are getting the Word, but we are not getting revelation. We are getting praise and worship, but we are not getting revelation. We are getting participation, but there is not revelation. We can choose when we hear a sermon, or hear a song, but God decides when the revelation shows up.

This is why it is important for everybody in the church to constantly stay engaged. You may hear a sermon in January, but the revelation may not come until June of that year. For example, I was in a Bible study recently, and all my life I have heard, the scripture, Foxes have holes, birds have nest, but the Son of Man has nowhere to lay His head (Matt. 8:20). But it wasn't until I was teaching a class on Acts 2, that one of my senior members, Sister Teresa McCullough, gave me one of the most thought-provoking revelations of that scripture I have ever heard. I was teaching in that class that the body of Christ didn't form until Acts 2 on the day of Pentecost, the birthday of the church. It was after Bible study that she came to me and said,

"Bishop, now it makes sense why Jesus didn't have anywhere to lay His head in the Gospel, because His body wasn't formed until Acts." She said, "Could it have been that he was saying, spiritually I have nowhere to rest my head, because my body has not been formed yet?" While some may consider this a theological stretch, it hit me right in my sweet spot. What revelation! In Acts, the head and the body now come together!

Revelation sees a prostitute coming and says that a future praise team leader is emerging. A drug dealer on the street may be revealed as a future deacon, who just doesn't know it yet. Revelation can also allow God to reveal who people are before we put them in leadership and staff positions where they actually run people out of the church. Revelation is helpful because if we pray for it, and ask God for it, God will show us His plan, and make it clear according to His word. If we are going to get Sunday Morning back, we must embrace the importance of relying upon revelation to enhance our self-esteem.

Miracles

Not only should we embrace holiness and revelation, but we must also embrace miracles. A miracle is when the supernatural supersedes the natural. How do you have low self-esteem when you have a God who is able to perform miracles? Low self-esteem can set in on Sunday Morning when we stop demonstrating and even stop preaching about the ability of God to perform miracles. The world needs to know that God can still work miracles.

The Bible tells us that all the books in the world couldn't record all the miracles that Jesus Christ did (John 21:25). It probably comes as no surprise that Jesus is considered the number one healer. He revived the dead, healed the sick and took a small portion of food and fed thousands. Scripture describes at least 39 miracles that Jesus performed during His public ministry, and various other miracles that are associated with Him, such as His birth, Transfiguration, Resurrection and Ascension. But don't think these were the only miracles that Jesus performed during His ministry.

When was the last time you heard a miracle testimony? When was the last time you gave a miracle testimony? When was the last time you encouraged a miracle testimony?

In conclusion, if we are going to take back Sunday Morning, it is important that the church believes in itself. The church is attractive, beautiful, and wonderful in His sight. While all of this is by His grace, this is the image that we must portray to the world, and the world will soon begin to look for us on Sunday Morning.

Group Discussion for Sunday Morning

1. What is your definition of low self-esteem?

2. What impact can low self-esteem have on the church?

3. What are the signs that a church may have low self-esteem?

4. What will be your recommendations for a church to deal with low-self esteem?

3

OUTDATED CHURCH
Stole Sunday Morning

"Forasmuch as ye know that ye were not redeemed with corruptible things, as silver and gold, from your vain conversation received by tradition from your fathers; But with the precious blood of Christ, as of a lamb without blemish and without spot:" –**1 Peter 1:18-19**

*I*n regards to what is happening in the fall away from the church today, it is imperative that we consider the role of "tradition" and "traditionalism." Jaroslav Pelikan once stated, "Tradition is the living faith of the dead; traditionalism is the dead faith of the living. And, I suppose I should add, it is traditionalism that gives tradition such a bad name." (Jaroslav Pelikan, *The Vindication of Tradition,* Yale University Press, 1984, p. 65). This very pointed statement about the differences in the two gives a clear picture as to what is happening with Sunday Morning in many of our churches.

Traditionalism is more connected to a spirit of being stuck, a spirit that lifts up whatever has already died, with the intent of giving it mouth-to-mouth resuscitation so that it can live again.

Some traditions of the church such as liturgy, hymns, observances, sacred ceremonies, in my opinion, we should never do away with. These things are connected to a story that exemplifies the faith of our Lord and Savior Jesus Christ! In other words, I still get inspired by revivals, Sunday School, and even singing songs like, "How Great Thou Art," and "What a Friend We Have in Jesus." These represent tradition at its best. We treat tradition as something that is taboo, but, think about it. Celebrating your birthday is tradition, and tradition is not a problem then. However, traditionalism is more connected to a spirit of being stuck, a spirit that lifts up whatever has already died, with the intent of giving it mouth-to-mouth resuscitation so that it can live again. The 100 Men in Black Program that only draws 24 men annually just might be dead. Can we put on black suits to bury it. While I know this may sound harsh and even sarcastic, many churches are dying for this very reason. They just refuse to have the funeral.

Let's Talk Sunday Morning– What Do We Do To Be Relevant?

Therefore, if Sunday Morning is going to thrive, we must begin to seriously consider making changes just so that we can survive. Oprah Winfrey once stated, "Doing the best at this moment, puts you in the best place for the next moment." John Legend said, "The future started yesterday and most of us are already too late." In other words, the church must move now, and make the upgrades to be effective. Recently, I had to upgrade my cell phone. While I had an Apple 6, I discovered that there were some features that I could not obtain until I upgraded to a 7 or even a 10. This speaks so profoundly to the movement of the church, if we are going to be effective at winning this war on Sunday Morning, we are going to have to upgrade, become relevant, and be conducive to change. Consider the areas that upgrades may need to happen in ministry.

Out Dated Language Must Go

In 2008, the European Parliament adopted gender-neutral language. This action means that as a culture,

Europeans are choosing to get rid of language that is exclusive and does not equally recognizes the other gender. Canada's Department of Justice changed lyrics in its national anthem "O Canada" to replace "all thy sons" with "all of us." Their reasoning was it is not only respectful, but it is also more accurate.

In 2013, the Washington Governor Jay Inslee signed a law in his state to adopt gender-neutral language. The law was part of a six-year effort by the state to pour through their legislation, replacing words like "fisherman" with "fisher."

Berkeley, California is doing away with "manholes," as "maintenance holes." "Firemen" in Berkeley will become "firefighters," and "man-made" will be "artificial" and all instances of "men and women" will be replaced by "people."

If Sunday Morning is going to take on meaning today, it is imperative that language is considered as it pertains to communicating the faith. We must constantly upgrade our language and how we communicate if we are going take Sunday Morning back from the enemy. For an example, there was a time when you could say "mankind," and everyone in the congregation knew that you were talking about humanity. However today, "man-kind" is so exclusive towards men that women feel completely left out. One Sunday after preaching I stated, "The doors of the church are open." There was an unchurched gentleman sitting in church that turned around, and was literally looking for the back doors of the church to open. He didn't know that I meant, it is time to make a decision about Christ, a change or a church home. That's exactly what I should have said. We must get rid of outdated language if we are going to save Sunday Morning.

It is important to understand that language and words matter, and how we use them can help us to win Sunday Morning back or further push people away from Sunday all together. Therefore, we must emphasize the importance of speaking in a way that people are included and not excluded. How does the ministry speak about singles, married couples, people who have been incarcerated, those of another race, or those who have a different sexual preference? Our language must always be respectful of other peoples' opinions, never demeaning or embarrassing, always with truth wrapped in love, and for the sole purpose to edify the worshipper while glorifying God. Language also plays a part in how we communicate our faith. While it is impressive to know the language of the faith, and expression of the church, never underestimate the power of "breaking it down" for people to understand and know exactly what you are talking about. Remember, everybody didn't grow up in church, and sometimes an explanation after a statement is sometimes necessary for understanding.

Examples of Language That Needs to Be Replaced

Old Language	New Language
• Him	God
• Mankind	Humanity
• Doors of the Church are Open	In Need of Christ a Church, or Change
• Visitors Please Stand	All are Welcomed

Let's Talk Sunday Morning– How Do We Upgrade The Church?

Style Is Like An Opinion-Everybody Has One

Perhaps we have lost some on Sunday Morning because we have negated the power of diversity in our style. Many pastors, leaders, choirs, ministry operations have one style of functioning, and they believe that everybody else should conform to that style. However, the church is so diverse today with church exposure, education, socio-economic levels, political views, races, etc., that we can no longer function with one style. Preachers must begin taking a different approach to how the message is conveyed, and every now and then change up style for effective communication. One Sunday the preacher may be inclined to preach a narrative sermon where passion and revelation ignites into shouting and praise. The next week the preacher may use more of a conversational approach to probe thought and action towards life changing decisions. One week the choir may sing in robes and hymns, but the next week the church may experience millennials singing in jeans, suspenders, and bow-ties with music that might be quite repetitive in lyric. Both styles communicate the Gospel, but one is more approachable than the other depending on generation. If Sunday Morning is to be re-discovered, the consideration of style is such that everybody does not learn, hear, and experience church the same way and a variety of approaches must be considered.

Message Stays the Same-Methodology Changes

If I were to go to a car dealership today and ask to purchase a car that had an 8-track player in it, no doubt I would get a strange look from the salesman considering that perhaps the salesman under 35 perhaps doesn't even know what an 8-track player is. We are living in a Spotify, Mp3, Music Download culture that makes the accessibility to music unprecedented. While the music on the 8-Track Player and the download feature may be the same, the method of playback is different. One is the old format, and the other is a new format. Same message, different methodology.

This becomes the challenge for us as we seek to take back Sunday Morning. We must not have our ministries to pigeonhole how we do church, but rather celebrate the fact that the message of Jesus Christ is on blast. The disadvantage that the church has to the world, is that the world is presented with many more venues and options for promoting its perverted message. The church in some way has limitations since its main venue is the church, but we must find ways to maximize the platform. Maximizing this platform means the church must be creative, and add spice to Sunday Morning. Be open for the arts, drama ministries, rap groups, media technology, dramatizations, and other creative forms of communicating to win souls to Christ. The message must stay the same, but how we present the Word, how we package the message, has to change.

Don't Let Outdated Church Steal Sunday Morning

It is important that if we are going to take Sunday Morning back, we must be open to change that can make us better. It was a wise writer, Fulton Oursler, who once stated, "Many of us crucify ourselves between two thieves—regret for the past and fear of the future." It is momentous that the changes you need to make in the ministry, you make now so that the two thieves won't steal your past or your future.

If there is a ministry that is doing something you desire, learn from that ministry and grow. Never be envious about the progress of another; that person could just be making a trail for you. You will never attract the anointing that you are jealous of or choose not to celebrate. Updating your perspective of God requires you to be open and flexible, and to possess a growth mindset to make changes that make a positive difference. You may look at a ministry and have doubts that you could be as effective as that minister. However, a growth mindset reminds you to give yourself the opportunity to learn and develop. You may not have that skill at this time, but God and time will bring about a change. While I believe we should be married to our core convictions, at some point, our convictions serve as spiritual launching pads that propel us into new ways of examining the state of the church. In doing this, we become intentional about God, we are more inclined to seeing God, and experiencing God who is always inviting us to draw close to Him. From being intentional about hearing and heeding God's Words, I believe Sunday Morning will become an experience, and not merely another stop.

- A recent study conducted by Pew Research Center provides additional interesting information on this topic. Pew researchers gave a sample of those who go to church at least once or twice a month, and gave a long list of potential reasons for attending. Pew's list combined tangible factors like sermons with intangible benefits such as getting closer to God. The results show that churchgoers rate three intangibles (to become closer to God, to become a better person, and for comfort in times of trouble and sorrow) at the top of the list, along with providing a moral foundation for children. Hearing valuable sermons comes in just below, in fifth place.

• The research I've reviewed here does not demonstrate conclusively that church leaders are an important factor in the decline in church attendance. There are many ongoing social and cultural changes that are affecting all aspects of Americans' lives, including religious attitudes and behaviors. But there can be little doubt that outstanding ministers who deliver powerful sermons, who have a warm and caring attitude toward their congregants, and who can manage the church well are critical factors in maintaining and increasing attendance at their places of worship.

• Many ministers may dislike the conclusion that they are personally responsible for attendance, and many may feel that expanding church attendance is not their primary ministerial goal. But, like it or not, pastors, priests and rabbis have accepted the mantle of responsibility for their church, and without engaged members, any church can wither away and literally be forced to close its doors.

Why They Don't Attend:

- "The things that keep people away from religious services are more complicated," wrote Pew researchers.

- Only 1 in 3 American adults who do not attend religious services (defined by Pew as attending a few times a year or less) say a very important reason is because they are not believers (28%). More say they practice their faith in other ways (37%) or they haven't found a church or other house of worship that they like (23%). About 1 in 5 say they don't like the sermons (18%) or cite logistical problems (22%).

Group Questions About Sunday Morning

1. What are some things about you, you need to change, but refuse to change?

   _____

   _____

   _____

2. What are some things in the ministry you feel may be outdated? _____

   _____

   _____

3. If you had to make some changes in a process, what will be your first five moves?

_____

_____

_____

4. When was a time you made changes and regretted doing so? And when was a time you made changes and actually loved it?

_____

_____

_____

4

CONSUMERISM,
MATERIALISM, MALLS,
DEPARTMENT STORES, AND
ONLINE SHOPPING

Stole Sunday Morning

But seek ye first the kingdom of God, and his righteous-
ness; and all these things shall be added unto
you. –**Matthew 6:33**

*T*he R & B musical group the Commodores, recorded
a song years ago titled, "Easy" led by Lionel Richie. There
is a lyric in that song when Richie says, "easy like Sunday
Morning." The question is – What is the meaning of "Easy
Like Sunday Morning" by the Commodores? The song
speaks about the release and the freedom from a really bad

relationship where the male in the relationship has paid his dues, did all he could to make it work, and now he realizes that the season has come for him to leave. There is liberation in knowing that you have done all you can do, and you get to a place where you can "lay your burdens down." So in essence what Richie is saying is when you have done your best, it's "easy" like Sunday Morning. "Easy" from the angle of when you have worked all week, did chores on Saturday, Sunday becomes a day of rest, worship, without schedule, without burden.

Before Sunday Mornings became busy with consumerism and commercialization, Sunday Mornings were set to be easy. Worship was the central focus for any culture and community, and it just seemed as if there was an easy calm that resonated because most people were found in church. "U.S. church membership was 70% or higher from 1937 through 1976, falling modestly to an average of 68% in the 1970s through the 1990s. The past 20 years have seen an acceleration in the drop-off, with a 20-percentage-point decline since 1999 and more than half of that change occurring since the start of the current decade." If you were to follow these numbers, it appears that this decline follows the implementation of laws that were changed to permit shopping on Sunday Morning.

When "blue laws" were in full effect, it was much easier to explain why nothing would be done on Sunday Morning except for the family to go to church. Sunday "blue laws" date all the way back to the colonial period, and it is a name that refers to the law that would make it mandatory that shopping centers and malls be closed on Sundays for the purpose of rest and worship. After years of Sundays being described in the words of Lionel Richie's, "Easy," Sunday Mornings took a shift and they became as busy as the next day. These laws began to be repealed in the 1960's, hence, giving rise to the freedom of Sunday Morning to be expressed openly and without retrieval. These laws were held so close to the chest that in 1961, the State of Maryland released the laws and allowed department stores to open, but you could only purchase tobacco products, such as candy, milk, bread, fruit, gasoline, oils, drugs, medicines, newspapers, and magazines. Any sale of items not on this list could result in penalties.

Sunday Mornings took a shift and they became as busy as the next day.

The changes in New York date from June 17, 1976, when the State Court of Appeals ruled that the state's blue laws forbidding the sale of most items on Sunday were unconstitutional. Judge Sol Wachtler, writing the decision for the seven-member court, said the hodge-podge of exceptions around the state made the laws irrational. Considerable opposition to the ruling was expressed by the New York State Council of Retail Merchants, religious leaders including Terence Cardinal Cooke of the New York Archdiocese, and many small merchants in the five boroughs. But within 10 weeks of the ruling, four of the five largest retailers in the city opened on Sunday for the first time, followed shortly by other large competitors and many small stores.

The other big stores joined in the Sunday openings immediately after Thanksgiving Day with the beginning of the Christmas shopping season. In New York, retailers said they initially realized a business gain of as much as 15% a week from Sunday openings. But as seven-day operations became standard, the weekly sales increment was reduced by more than half and then by two-thirds, as business on Saturday and especially on Monday reflected inroads from the Sunday openings.

It was not long after this that shopping on Sunday Morning would spread not only throughout the nation, but it continued to spread throughout the world. Today, shopping on Sunday Morning or even preparing to go shopping on Sunday Morning is an all too normal thing to do.

Consider these interesting facts about consumerism on Sunday Morning, and perhaps why many people are not found to be in church.

Sunday Morning is one of the busiest shopping days of the week behind Monday morning. Mondays generated over 16% of weekly revenue on average, and a large portion of that being online. Revenue generated on Mondays is 10% higher than Sunday, the second best revenue generator. The explanation has been that people typically work throughout the week. On the weekend, time is spent with family at soccer games, various outings, events, and family time. Sunday Morning has become a day to prepare for work week, therefore, more grocery shopping, mall shopping, even hardware shopping takes place on Sunday Morning. While it is illegal to buy cars in 14 states in the United States on Sunday Morning, this is simply because of the appearance of salesmen competing against one another on a Sunday Morning not being a good look. This does not negate the idea that many people take Sunday Morning to just drive from car lot to car lot to simply look at cars, and then perhaps buy them within the week.

Sunday Morning Shopping is Interrupting Rest

The notion of consumerism and commercialization has made shopping the new model of finding rest and restoration on Sunday Morning. Recently, I saw a quote that said, "Sunday, a day to refuel your soul and be grateful for your blessings. Take a deep breath and relax. Enjoy your family, your friends, and a cup of coffee." Notice, that while this thought mentions blessings, it mentions nothing about being in church. This is the mindset that many people have adopted today, and this is how the enemy is stealing Sunday Morning. You have to be intentional with your Sunday Morning. You have to be intentional about refueling your soul in worship, and being grateful for your blessings in the house of the One who blessed you. Sunday Morning is more than just taking a deep breath, it is using your breath to give God the glory, and relaxing in His glory. It's one thing to enjoy your family and friends, and it's another thing to be in church with them beside you. Many churches are inviting coffee in sanctuaries as means to create an environment of conversation. I'm not suggesting for or against, however I am for whatever it takes to get people back in the sanctuary on Sunday Morning. There are times when we have to make adjustments for this to happen.

Sunday Morning Shopping Is Taking Church Money

Not only has consumerism and commercialization tapped into the rest factor, but it has also tipped up on the generosity teaching of the church. Sunday Morning is typically a giving day for Christians. If the enemy can lure Christians from the church into the stores without changing their patterns and their passion for giving, the enemy has not only stolen Sunday Morning, but he has stolen the money too. The money that they would have been putting in the offering plate or giving on Push Pay, or to Givelify, is now going in the cash register at the mall. No wonder there are so many churches that are facing shut down, foreclosures, sale of properties and buildings, because as Sunday Mornings draw more people out of church to other forms of recreation, so, too, goes the finances that lends way to supporting the budget.

Sunday Morning Shopping Is Taking Seniors and Millennials

This is not a factual statement in terms of statistics and data, but merely observation. As a pastor I have noticed that there is a segment of my membership missing from any given Sunday. When I inquire about where they have been, more often than not, many respond by saying, "I'm working on Sundays now. I have not left the church, but I'm just working trying to get mine." This is all too popular, that millennials, young adults and seniors, are working two and three jobs just to survive. Unfortunately, many of their work schedules have them busy on Sunday Morning, which does not give them adequate time for worship. If the stores are open on Sundays, somebody has to open the doors.

Let's Talk Sunday Morning

How Do We Get People Out of Stores, Offline, and Back in Church?

1. Instruct churches on what it means to keep the Sabbath holy.

2. Encourage members to attend worship before they go to the malls and shopping centers.

3. Instruct Christians that it is their right to tell their employers that worship is part of their religion, and they need Sunday Morning time given for worship.

4. Encourage members to budget their finances, and know the difference between needs and wants. Finances are a major part of church vision and momentum, and are much needed to finance the work of the Kingdom.

5. Consider alternate days for worship. While this writing is about Sunday Morning, if you can't get them on Sunday Morning, consider alternate worship service times and perhaps even have worship on Thursday nights or Saturday mornings.

Questions To Take Back Sunday

1. What is it that is keeping you out of church on Sunday Morning? _____

   _____

   _____

2. Do you shop on Sundays, and what realization does that give you?

   _____

   _____

   _____

3. What way can a person tell their employer that worship is a priority for them on Sunday Mornings, and work is not an option?

   _____

   _____

   _____

4. Would you risk losing a job opportunity for this very purpose?_____

   _____

   _____

5

AAU BASKETBALL, SOCCER, DANCE RECITALS, AND OTHER SPORTS

Stole Sunday Morning

If any of you lack wisdom, let him ask of God, that giveth to all men liberally, and upbraideth not; and it shall be given him. **–James 1:5**

We have the Youth Character Football League organized and sponsored by our ministry. It is a league geared toward developing integrity and character, while ultimately impacting football players, cheerleaders, coaches, and players with the love of Christ. Our director came to me on one occasion and said to me that the league that we are now a part of is desiring for our team to play on a Sunday

Morning at 11:00 A.M. Needless to say, my blood pressure shot through the roof, my head started spinning, and before I knew it, I came out of my shirt like the incredible hulk. While this is a tongue in cheek exaggeration of my response, I was very stern and almost angered in my protest of this by saying no, and even threatening to pull us immediately out of this league. My question to him was, " How are we going to allow the enemy to take children out of the church on a Sunday Morning, and put a football in their hands? Is that going to solve the sin problem that they will face in this life?" This is the reality of what we are dealing with when we allow sports and recreation to take our young people and their families out of church on Sunday Mornings.

The Impact of AAU and other
Sunday Morning Sports

While sports have always been a major part of development for many youth, the game went to another level when competition shifted from weekdays and Saturdays to Sunday Mornings. The Amatuer Athletic Union (AAU) Basketball League is most notable for shooting hoops on Sunday Morning; in order to understand the evolution of this, it is momentous to know the history of AAU.

Amateur Athletic Union has been around since 1888. The establishment of this organization has been attributed to two founders because of the discrepancy in recorded history. The two names mentioned are; James E. Sullivan and William Buckingham Curtis. The mere fact that its very own history can't be attributed to one founder could speak to the foundation of AAU breeding some division for families, churches and communities on Sunday Mornings. In the past, AAU served in the capacity of giving young people hope for sporting dreams after college, while also preparing athletes for Olympic opportunities. After the Amateur Sports Act of 1978 broke up the AAU's responsibility as the national Olympic sports governing body, the AAU focused on providing sports programs for all participants of all ages beginning at the local and regional levels. AAU is dedicated exclusively to the promotion and development of amateur sports and physical fitness programs. It has more than 700,000 members nationwide, including more than 100,000 volunteers.

AAU really saw peak development in the late 80's and the early 90's when the focus went away from talent development and coaching skills for performance, to marketing and branding teams and players for corporate sponsorship. Here is how it works: a volunteer coach decides he wants a team, he recruits the top players in his region, district or community, the coach then appeals to shoe companies like Nike, Adidas, Reebok, and Under Armor. The idea is for the team to be ranked in such a way nationally, that one of these companies would sponsor the team with shoes, uniforms, bags, and other travel gear. But the hidden agenda to this is the hope that perhaps one of these "uprising super-star players" will make it big in college and the NBA. It is the company's idea that once they arrive at the professional level, the once AAU super star will still wear their shoe in the NBA. So AAU all comes down to somebody's S-O-N making it to the N-B-A to wear S-H-O-E-S.

The Challenge with AAU on Sunday Morning

AAU nationally has had a major impact on Sunday Morning. When a young person is playing basketball on a Sunday Morning at worship time, the worship is not just missing that youth. But consider when these teams play on Sunday Mornings at 11:00 A.M., often times the entire family goes to support, which means that there may be an entire family that is missing from worship because of a game on Sunday Morning. Not to mention, if that young man is "a baller," it is possible that not only does the family leave church to see him play, but friends will often follow. We speak as if the youth playing the sports male, because AAU traditionally has not been open for female engagement in this regard.

Consider some interesting insights about AAU Sports before engaging your child in this capacity.

1. Many youth play AAU Basketball because it is believed that many college scouts and coaches watch them closer in this venue. However, if that young person is able to play school ball and play it well, the same college scouts and coachers will see them there as well.

2. Many parents can't afford the cost of AAU, and often go broke trying to keep their youth traveling and supporting their activities by renting vehicles, hotel rooms, flight tickets, and other expenses that often put a strain on families. School ball is free, and many of these expenses are removed.

3. Many professional "ballers" who played AAU will confess that if you want your youth to be well-coached and developed, AAU is not always the best option. Many coaches are not required to have any formal coaching training or development for coaching. Many have classified AAU as a "high-speed pick-up game." Consider what some of the greats had to say about AAU Basketball.

Steve Kerr:

"Teams play game after game after game, sometimes winning or losing four times in one day. Very rarely do teams ever hold a practice. Some programs fly in top players from out of state for a single weekend to join their team. Certain players play for one team in the morning and another one in the afternoon. If mom and dad aren't happy with their son's playing time, they switch club teams and stick him on a different one the following week. The process of growing as a team basketball player — learning how to become part of a whole, how to fit into something bigger than oneself — becomes completely lost within the AAU fabric."

Kobe Bryant:

"AAU basketball. Horrible, It's stupid. It doesn't teach our kids how to play the game at all, so you wind up having players that are big and they bring it up and they do all this fancy crap and they don't know how to post. They don't know the fundamentals of the game. It's stupid."

Gregg Popovich:

"Ever since AAU became the de facto leader in 'preparing kids', it's been all downhill."

Charles Barkley:

"This new generation, they all stick together. They all play together, and they're all AAU babies. Any type of criticism directed toward them, they consider it hate. Even if it's a fair criticism, they consider it hate. So no, it does not bother me what the new generation thinks, to be honest with you. I know they all stick together, so that's just part of it, too."

While there are many cons to playing AAU, there are also some positives. It is a good thing that youth who may live in remote areas where coaches do not travel to regularly can be seen on a national level. Some players have received full scholarships as a result of their participation in AAU basketball, and some have stayed out of gangs and other forms of violence as result of their involvement. Therefore, we should not be against AAU all together; we should find ways to direct AAU activity from being a distraction on Sunday Mornings.

Let's Talk Sunday Morning–

How Do We Get Youth Off of Basketball Courts and Back Into the Church On Sunday Morning?

Since AAU is a multi-million dollar operation, it is going to be very difficult for the Church to do anything to stop that forward movement of AAU, nor should this be our intent. We just simply want families to not have to choose between church and AAU Basketball. What can we do to get youth off of the courts on Sunday Morning, and back in the church where true transformation can happen? And, if a person chooses to engage with AAU, here are some things that should strongly be considered.

Boycott Sunday Morning Play– It would be helpful if pastors and church leaders could call a meeting with AAU teams in the local community, and discuss the concerns with Sunday Morning play time. Perhaps one could suggest having games to be played on Sunday after 2:00 P.M., when most worship services have concluded.

Preach and Teach Affordability– While all youth deserve investment, make sure parents are aware of the fees associated with AAU, and can afford the cost of travel and the cost that goes along with this sport. This cost may take a toll on church offering, therefore, classes on budgeting and showing the impact on loss of income because of activities like AAU are essential.

Provide Basketball Leagues With Good Coaching– If basketball is a main attraction for youth, then churches should begin to start basketball leagues as a means of evangelism. However, find trained coaches that can teach technique and one who understands the function of the game for affectability.

Games vs Practices– Find a team that has one or two practices a week, and preferably a team that puts emphasis on character development, local travel, and concern for family time.

In closing, while AAU has become the primary focus of this chapter, this form of escapism from the church also finds its way through dance recitals, cheerleading competitions, soccer games, and even NFL day trips. It is important that we stand up as a collective voice, and speak out in disassociation and protest against these groups that are taking our children out of church and putting them on game fields Sunday Morning at 11:00 A.M.

Sunday Morning Group Questions

1. Have you ever been pressured to put your child in a sporting activity on Sunday Morning, and how did you handle it?

2. How many AAU teams are in your city, and how feasible will it be to call a meeting with those teams to discuss these matters?

_____

_____

_____

3. What could be the result if we are able to get these families back in the church?

_____

_____

_____

4. How effective do you think a Bible study would be on the impact of AAU?

_____

_____

_____

6

PATHETIC POLITICS IN THE WHITE CHURCH AND THE BLACK CHURCH

Stole Sunday Morning

Let every soul be subject unto the higher powers. For there is no power but of God: the powers that be are ordained of God. **–Romans 13:1**

Why Young People Are Leaving The White Church

*T*his is the reality that hits home when I read an article in Newsweek Magazine titled, *Evangelical Christians Helped Elect Donald Trump, but Their Time as a Major Political Force Is Coming to an End* by Nina Burleigh. This article was never intended to be about promoting one political party over another; however, this political maneuver by the evangelical church has an epic impact on culture, and merits us to look at how this move is affecting Sunday Morning, particularly in the white evangelical church and other churches alike.

It is no secret that today the white evangelical church is fighting for the re-establishment of relevance, integrity, and definition as they face the fallout from 80% of them voting for and supporting the Trump administration. "Since the 1970s, white evangelicals have formed the backbone of the Republican base. But as younger members reject the vitriolic partisanship of the Trump era and leave the church, that base is getting smaller and older. The numbers are stark: Twenty years ago, just 46 percent of white evangelical Protestants were older than 50; now, 62 percent are above 50. The median age of white evangelicals is 55. Only 10 percent of Americans under 30 identify as white evangelicals. The exodus of those under 30 is so swift that demographers now predict that evangelicals will likely cease being a major political force in presidential elections by 2024."

The religious right and the republican party really goes all the way back to 1954, to the Supreme Court ruling of Brown vs. the Board of Education of Topeka. This ruling put it front and center for public schools to be desegregated, which would ultimately cause outbreak and protest particu-

larly in the Southern regions of America. In the South, the
GOP opened up exclusive singular racial schools (white),
backed by tax-exempt status, that would promote prohibit-
ing their children from going to schools with blacks. These
schools, largely religious in nature, would be tax-exempt
until the IRS began to challenge their rights and privileges
to be tax-exempt but promote separatism. A big-time
Republican Paul Weyrich pulled in Joseph Coors-the beer
mogul, and they began to lobby and partner with preachers
like Jerry Falwell and other conservative pastoral leaders
for voice and power. Falwell's intent was for schools to
remain an entity for separatism, while get government
money to help them. This became one of the first major
moves of what we know as the "Moral Majority" that really
launched its presence in the 80's with the backing of Ronald
Reagan. Dr. Samuel Dewitt Proctor, in one of his prophetic
critiques of the church, said, "for any group to call themselves "the moral majority" is in and of itself "immoral."
With his uncanny way he would say, "who walks around
and says, 'look at me, I'm moral.' Nevertheless, this movement was birthed, and their alignment of church and politics
was strong, adopting as predominant principle issues like
"gun-control" and "abortion."

Now their children's children are disgruntled, and are
leaving their side all because of their opposition to this

party that is standing with the Trump administration. Little of this has to do with a political party, but their quandary is how do you call yourself "moral," but elect a president who is thrice-married, a foul-mouthed mogul with a history of sexual assault, and one who supports from the side-line, white supremacy. His brand will forever be stained for caging children, and spewing personal "bully" assaults on anyone who does not think like him, act like him, or function as he does. More than 80 percent of the evangelical vote put him in office in 2016.

But Paul Tillich says " if you want to know a person's true religion, we ought to ask about a person's "ultimate concern."

Stephen Mansfield in his book, *Choosing Donald Trump* gives hint as to how the GOP elected one that does not necessarily promote their morals, when he said that it is not so much that Trump is "informing" America, but he is "revealing" America. While Trump was raised a Presbyterian, many of his supporters will say that his faith is personal. Critics say that he has no religion, but Paul Tillach says " if you want to know a person's true religion, we ought to ask about a person's "ultimate concern." Hence, it is obvious for many of the younger generation who are angry with their parents and grandparents for supporting Trump, that his concern is not religion, but "self-winning: "being rich", and "being the best" (*Choosing Donald Trump,* p. 72).

This philosophy has killed Sunday Morning for many of the younger generation desiring to follow the blue-print of the GOP. Their choice now is to reject this administrative position by leaving the evangelical church or at least not attending on Sunday Mornings. Ed Setzer gave revelation to what is going on with youth primarily of the white evangelical church, and why they are not attending church when he revealed these findings:

- (27 percent) simply wanted a break from church.
- (25 percent) moved to college.
- (23 percent) said that work made it impossible or difficult to attend.
- (26 percent) felt that church members seemed judgmental or hypocritical.
- (20 percent) didn't feel connected to the people at their church.
- (15 percent) expressed that church members were unfriendly and unwelcoming.
- (52 percent) indicated some sort of religious, ethical or political beliefs as the reason they dropped out.

While all of these statistics are startling, what is the mind-blower for me is the 52 percent of this group that indicated disappointment with the church because of "religious, ethical, or political belief." Robert McCarty, one of the study's authors, told the audience that about a third of respondents left over church teaching, most often that on same-sex marriage and homosexuality. "Young people see dealing with the gay community as an issue of social justice and human dignity, not an issue of sexuality." he said. There is no way the GOP cannot see these numbers, and directly relate it to their support of an administration that does not uphold the younger generations perspective of race, sexuality, relationships, and the need for diversity and globalization. Hence, many of them are missing on Sunday Morning, and refuse to come and hear a gospel that does more of "shaming people" than "saving people." If these matters are not mentioned on Sunday Morning, what is equally difficult for them to swallow, is no mentioning of these "inhumane policies" that, in their minds, are putting the lives of people in turmoil.

Why Young People Are Leaving The Black Church

While most of the flight from churches in the white community are directly related to the issue of "political relevance," the black church is in trouble with its youth because of issues related to integrity and the merging of other religions. Consider some of the reasons that young African-Americans are leaving the black church.

Traditionalism and Relevance

Many African-American youth and young adults will confess that they are leaving church because of traditionalism. They will say things like, "people don't want to change;" "they are not open for how we function and think;" "the church has been the same since I was a child." Many churches are missing these youth on Sunday Morning because they simply don't want to change. If the church is going to reverse this thinking, it is important that we rethink how we are doing church, and involve youth in the goals and objectives of the church.

Social Justice Issues

For many African-American youth, social justice is a major priority. There are many problems that ail the African-American community such as, gang crime, gun violence, domestic matters, depression, communal trauma, drugs and crime just to name a few. However, the Black Lives Matter movement started outside of the Black Church because many felt that the church was not doing enough and not speaking to the issues. As a result, many of them have become disgruntled with the church and are now allowing voices outside of the church, namely; rap artists from the hip-hop community, to be their voice to truth and power. If Sunday Morning for many of these youth is to be realized again, pulpits must begin to shift their theology and incorporate social-justice matters into their messages, and stand for the human dignity of all people.

Rise of New Religious Forms

There is an emergence of new interpretive religious expression happening in the "Black Church," and it involves the diversity in how religion is expressed. Consider some of the religious and spiritual formations that are all too popular in the African-American community today.

- **Nation of Islam**

  There is a new thinking of church today, and much of it has nothing to do with Jesus. Back in the 60's and early 70's, the biggest threat at that time to the church was the teaching and preaching of Elijah Muhammad with the Nation of Islam. This religion came in with a hard message for mainstream America to receive, which was the message that the "white man" was not to be trusted, and people of color had the answers to their own problems. According to C. Eric Lincoln, Sociologist of Religion, they believed that the white man's day had passed, and there was no need to integrate with him since his day was done. " They taught that the black race needed a new morale, economic self-sufficiency, a high code of personal morals, and a return to the pristine glory of their race. Lincoln suggested that the black man needed to free himself from all remnants of slave mentality and from Christianity which has too long kept him doped in subservience to the white man. (Lincoln, Black Muslims in America, p. 3).

This was quite different from the traditional form of the "black Sunday Morning experience," where all of our belief system hinged on our deliverance found in Jesus. The Nation of Islam sees Jesus as a mere prophet, while Christians saw Jesus as their Savior. This message has resonated with many African-American males that are incarcerated. This message of identity, self-empowerment, and boldness comes across well with this population, and more often than not, these men may go in with "Jesus," but come out with "Muhammad."

- **African Spiritualism**

Luna Malbroux in her recent article, *Why More Young Black People Are Trading Church For African Spirituality,* reveals that although black Americans still tend to be more religious than the general population, those under 30 are three times as likely to avoid religious affiliation than black people over the age of 50. She goes on to suggest that while black young adults are leaving organized religion, or what we know as "good Sunday Morning church," they are embracing African spirituality. African spirituality for many of them does not require the formality of God.

This kind of spirituality is very much laid back, does not require much reasoning, has no demand for new member classes, evangelism work, prayer calls, or the guilt of not winning a soul to Christ. Perhaps somewhere in this objection is the break away from formal dress as a code for worship. On the contrary, African spirituality is promoting meditation, reiki, acupuncture, sage, and herbal tinctures to increase self-care and the dealing with grief and trauma. It is not uncommon to find one who embraces this spirituality, to often burn candles with shrines of African gods, and embrace self-empowerment by the ancestors of the past and present.

This form of spirituality has become attractive to many black young adults because they believe that the Christian culture continues to uphold patriarchy, a rape culture, and white supremacy—even within black churches. This is what gave way for Beyonce's *Lemonade* to get many nods towards African spirituality. "Weaved within the movements for black lives are spiritual and ritualistic resources, and how we understand oppression and destructive politics that keep its foot on the neck of the people. Through African Spirituality, we have learned not only the importance of reclaiming our time, but also our history, our spirits, and our joy."

- **The Illuminati**

  The Illuminati (plural of Latin *illuminatus,* "enlightened"). Historically, the name usually refers to the Bavarian Illuminati, an Enlightenment-era secret society founded on May 1, 1776. The society's goals were to oppose superstition, religious influence over public life, and abuses of state power. This is a new found religion for many black youth after popularized by many rap artist who ascribe to the belief system that God is not in control of the world, but the world is indeed governed by a secret society of elitists who are making decisions about globalization, the news, the economy, wars, and political moves in various countries.

- **Black Hebrew Israelites** (also called Black Hebrews, African Hebrew Israelites, and Hebrew Israelites) are groups of Black Americans who believe that they are the descendants of the ancient Israelites. At the end of the 19th century, Frank Cherry and William Saunders Crowdy both claimed that African-Americans were the descendants of Hebrews in the Bible. In the United States during the late 19th and early 20th centuries, from Kansas to New York City, African Americans and West Indian immigrants began to grow this group, and by the mid-1980s, the number of Black Hebrews in the United States was between 25,000 and 40,000.

Black Hebrews adhere to the religious beliefs and practices of both Christianity and Judaism. Those who did convert to Judaism, are not recognized as Jews by the greater Jewish community. Many choose to identify as Hebrew Israelites or Black Hebrews rather than Jews in order to indicate their claimed historic connections. Many young African-American men are leaving Christian churches and uniting with this front because of its strong look and the appreciation of knowledge that juxtaposes traditional Christian teaching.

- **Bedside Tabernacle**

Many black youth are not doing new movements, their new movement is simply another turnover in the bed. Many black youth are choosing a religion of self-empowerment, void of any preacher preaching to them because of their disappointment of activity and structure in the traditional Christian church. Their church is Sunday Morning video tournaments, basketball games on their favorite network, and they may pause for a moment to watch their favorite preacher on BET or Facebook live.

Let's Talk Sunday Morning–
How Do We Correct the Politics of the Church?

- If the White Church is to draw young people back to their churches, it is going to be imperative that they separate their theology from the religious right, and simply do what is right. In the future, an emergence of political issues will have to be addressed from the pulpit, not with the agenda of a presidential candidate, but with the agenda of Jesus Christ for which the Gospel is preached.

- If the Black Church is to win back its youth, it is going to be necessary that the church returns back to what Lincoln calls the "black sacred cosmos" where religious experience is witnessed during the moments of the sacred and the secular. Black youth are in a dire need for relevance, and relevance is often mastered in understanding the culture for which they exist. This is not to suggest that the church needs to embrace the multiplicity of religious forms, but we must learn to co-exist in a community where those forms are growing, while we still preach Jesus.

- Both the white and the black church must constantly look at traditionalism, and how old forms of church are in need of an upgrade. It is imperative that neither church would put their denominational dogma over the development of relationships and time spent with many young adults.

- Young people are looking for a religion that is real. For the white church the separation between the Bible that they read, and the behavior of President Donald Trump was a great inconsistency. In the black church the idea of praying to God on Sunday Morning, while not addressing issues such as kneeling before the flag, police brutality in the streets, black men and children being gunned down in the community, racial injustice everywhere you turn, and then come to church and hear no reference of these matters for black youth is a big turn off. Therefore, if Sunday Morning is to be realized, Sunday messages must be consistent with God's word, and practical with the times and their reality.

- What is interesting is that among white youth and black youth, there seems to be a radical redefinition of relationships. If the church is going to be effective in reaching this group and getting them back in the church on Sunday Morning, we must begin to accept the notion that relationships are being redefined, and the denial and acceptance of those who are is different than we are must be embraced and not just tolerated or worse yet ex-communicated. While God's word is true, the truest word of the entire Bible is His love.

Group Discussion Questions About Sunday Morning

1. Is there any policy in this church that is keeping youth and young adults away from the church?

2. Is it necessary to change what we are presently doing to reach the young generation?

3. What will happen if we don't make a deliberate effort to reach this generation of youth?

4. How open will you be for new paradigms and shifts in youth relationships?

_____

_____

_____

7

FALSE PROPHETS AND PULPIT IMMORALITY

Stole Sunday Morning

Beware of false prophets, which come to you in sheep's clothing, but inwardly they are ravening wolves. Ye shall know them by their fruits. Do men gather grapes of thorns, or figs of thistles? Even so every good tree bringeth forth good fruit; but a corrupt tree bringeth forth evil fruit. **–Matthew 7:15-20**

*I*t amazes me how many people refuse to come to church or are falling out of church because of their lack of confidence in the preacher. One wise preacher once said to me, "preachers will not only be responsible for the souls that they preach into heaven, but we will also be responsible for the souls we keep out of heaven."

False prophets and pulpit immorality is at an all-time high. The body of Christ is experiencing something today that is constantly lowering the bar of what Christianity should be, and what real deliverance looks like. It appears that as soon as someone senses a call to ministry, the next stop is the pulpit. However, ministry is much larger than the pulpit: it is about serving and being there as a representative of God, for the purpose of God getting all the glory.

False Prophets

False prophets are not new, they are as old as the biblical structure. However, the manifestation of their presentation often changes depending on time and culture. Consider these scriptures that reference false prophets:

- 'Beware of false prophets, for they come to you in sheep's clothing, but inwardly they are ravening wolves'. (Mat. 7:15).

- These lick and suck the blood of souls: 'Beware of dogs, beware of evil workers, beware of the concision.' (Phil. 3:2).

- These kiss and kill; these Peace, peace, till souls fall into everlasting flames-Proverbs 7.

Signs of a False Prophet

1. False Teachers are People-Pleasers (Gal. 1:10; 1 Thess. 2:1-4).

One of the signs of a false prophet is one whose call is no deeper than the applause they get from the people. These are "crowd pleasers" that will use any theology, try any antic, promote any trend, just to please the crowd. These are preachers who are preaching what the "pew" desires, and not what God is truly saying.

Perhaps Sunday Mornings have been hit because there are many preachers who are preaching what the culture is demanding and not truly what God is saying. Could it be that Sunday Morning has been stolen because the God-conscious challenge of holiness, miracles, and revelation is gone, and has been replaced with theatrics that can't hold the spiritual appetite past Sunday brunch? Sunday Morning will comeback if preachers move from pleasing people, to pleasing God.

2. False Prophets Shame the People and Do Not Edify the People

Another sign of the false prophet is shaming people into loyalty, the faith, and in the body of Christ. Jesus always functioned from the position of love, and while He was at times very disciplined and stern with His approach,

His intent was to always win souls to Christ, and not push them away.

We are ministering to a culture that does not know church, and many in this culture were not raised in the church. In the words of the late Bishop G.E. Patterson, "we are now counseling what we once prayed deliverance over." The church once rebuked behavior like drinking, smoking, and shacking. There was a time when great emphasis was placed on the length of dress, make-up, and other things that have nothing to do with the kingdom. These "rebukes" are no longer considered God, but today it will be deemed as "rude," to correct people in the church.

If we are going to win back people to Sunday morning, it is important that we established correction and order

If we are going to win back people to Sunday Morning, it is important that we establish correction and order with biblical paradigm, with concern, with love, and not the spirit of a curse. Prophets are called to edify the body of Christ, and not to shame them.

3. False Prophets and Teachers Are Notable For Exposing Others Who Serve With Them In Ministry

It seems that only in the church do we find people who are on the same team, ganging up on others who are on the same team. What will it look like for a football player to tackle his own teammate during the super bowl? What would it look like for a fire fighter to put a fire fighter in the fire? These images should bring it home to other preachers and prophets, that this is what it looks like for clergy to fight one another. The Word of God declares, one plants, Apollos waters, but it is God who gives the increase (I Cor 3:6-8). All of us don't have the same assignment, but we all have a place in the Kingdom. Jesus put it this way when John had concern about others casting out demons, He said, "if they are not against us, they are for us (Mark 9:39).

If we are going to win souls back to Sunday Morning, it is imperative that pastors, teachers, evangelists, prophets, and ministers show a consolidated front. Yes, in the kingdom of God there will always be differences; however, those differences should be kept among ourselves, and not exposed on social media or any other formats to the people for whom we are trying to reach.

4. False Teachers use Clever Language and Slick Approaches To Ministry

Within the body of Christ there are some false prophets and teachers that use the church and ministry for personal gain. There are some who approach ministry almost with a "hoo-do effect," promising magical things to happen, when in reality they have no control over our destiny. God has always used the prophet to speak or forth-tell those things that are to happen in human history, but many false prophets today are using God's Word to fleece the people into making salvation something to be earned, and not simply experienced.

There are false prophets today who are making people feel guilty if they can't give personal items as offerings, sign over titles of property for the promise of a bigger blessing, or even loan them money for the purpose of investment into personal accounts. All these things are wrong, and have no place in the body of Christ. "So false teachers will put a great deal of paint and garnish upon their most dangerous principles and blasphemies, that they may the better deceive and delude poor ignorant souls. They eye your goods more than your good; and mind more the serving of themselves, than the saving of your souls. So they may have your substance, they care not though Satan has your souls (Rev. 18:11-13)."

If the church is going to make the vote for Sunday Morning return, there must be an assessment on how finances and money are handled in the church. This is not the season for the pastor to be the only one in the church with great profits, while the rest of the congregation struggle with keeping their lights on. We must be wise and get regular audits, announce the plan for accountability, give more than we take, and realize that there is always some-body like the I.R.S. that is watching.

Immorality of Preachers

Immorality among preachers is just not something that you expect, but today I believe that it is a contributing factor to who stole Sunday Morning. In the early 2000s, the Boston Globe revealed a major sting regarding Catholic priests who were caught sexually abusing children for years without consequences. This exposure was an eye-opener for the Catholic Church, and policy was put into place that would prohibit this from happening in the future. Nevertheless, they are still facing fallout from this grim reality. I must also add, that these scandals are found in protestant reformations as well. "The scandals aren't always as sinister as abuse though. Some pastors who claim to be clean as a whistle, on the straight and narrow, and happily devoted to their wives have turned out to be lying, cheating, or caught with gay prostitutes. These revelations can be particularly shocking," not to mention those who extort money from the members, caught stealing money from the collections on Sundays, or even those who have become so comfortable that the "night club bar" is known amongst his or her members as being their late-night pulpit.

I would be irresponsible in my writing if I did not put in print that there are many more preachers who live right than there are those who live wrong. As a matter of fact, you can count on one hand the scandals about preachers that you have heard about in your own city. If there are 400 churches in a city, there are perhaps one or two negative stories you may hear about concerning a pastor.

While it is important to recognize that there are dysfunctions among clergy and laity, the office of the preacher is still held to a higher standard considering that a call has been extended from the One who gives us power to overcome our dysfunction. I often say in teaching sessions, "we are all born with something, but Jesus said, 'we must be born again.' We preach salvation, but now the world is ready to see us live salvation. Sunday Morning is being impacted by the lack of integrity, and it is essential today that we restore it.

Let's Talk Sunday Morning-
How Do We Restore the Preacher?

Call Investigation– Perhaps one of the reasons that indiscretions are so popular in the pulpit today is because we are not doing the vetting that needs to be done to make certain that sincerity, understanding, maturity, and even ability is present before we present one to the pulpit.

Whatever happened to the days when churches and ministry councils really did put you on "trial" when you had to prove yourself to be fit for ministry? If Sunday Morning is going to be restored, we must begin to be more selective about who we grant ministry licenses to, and be more strategic about the preparation of ministry.

Accountability– If Sunday Morning is to be corrected by the preacher, it is important that accountability channels are put into place to help structure, council, direct, and even give pastors and ministers a place to be mentored. Presently, I serve as a Bishop in Global United Fellowship, and I am constantly requested to serve in the capacity of being a pastor to pastors. Because I realize that whatever any preacher does impacts the kingdom of God, I count it an honor to be able to speak truth into the lives of other pastors, but to also allow them to speak truth to me. This kind of accountability is needed, and you can't get an attitude, when somebody "calls you out," and tells you much better is expected.

Therapy– One of the corrective measures for pastors who may be living out of control, is the dire need and necessity for therapy. It is important that the church press the issue of theology and therapy going together. "A 2013 study by Lifeway Research found that nearly half of evangelicals "believed that people with serious mental disorders can overcome their illnesses with 'Bible study and prayer alone.'" "Serious mental disorders" include depression, bipolar disorder, and even schizophrenia—the three disorders most closely associated with suicide." What we now know is that Bible study and prayer alone are not enough, and there are times when even pastors need a trained therapist to help them deal with many of their problems and concerns.

Dethrone the Preacher

While this sounds like we are attacking the privileged place and power granted to the preacher, it is by no means to be a suggestion of disrespect. To speak of dethroning the preacher, is a reference to allowing the preacher to be human, and removing unrealistic expectations from his or her life. Preachers need to laugh: they need to share, and they need down time: they need to come out of the "collar." They need moments when they can cry, admit that they are hurting, be human, and most importantly, feel that you love them and support them.

It is important to know that if we are going to bring honor back to Sunday Morning, we must continue to give honor and support to our pastors and leaders. They are vital to what God wants to do in the earth realm, and God will continue to have a plan for pastors on Sunday Morning.

Group Questions To Discuss About Sunday Morning

1. How have you, in the past, given support to your pastor/leader?

_____

_____

_____

2. Why do you think some pastors fall from grace?

_____

_____

_____

3. What are some other ways we can help pastors remain whole while they minister the Gospel of Jesus Christ?

_____

_____

_____

4. Who is the most admirable pastor you know?

_____

_____

_____

8

SOCIAL MEDIA
Stole Sunday Morning

"And let us consider how to stir up one another to love and good works, not neglecting to meet together, as is the habit of some, but encouraging one another, and all the more as you see the Day drawing near."
–Hebrews 10:24-25

*W*hen social media hit the scene and new communal connectedness found its way in the church, those who missed church services would no longer have to order tapes. The audio and video ministry used to take a week to run the copies. The missionaries would pick up the recording the following Sunday, and depending on their own personal schedules the recordings would eventually get to the house of the sick and shut-in.

Social media has changed the game; particularly during the initial break of the Coronavirus. Since churches could not convene, social media is all we had to keep us connected. This is a game-changer because now worship and your connection to the ministry does not require you to do anything but scroll. While this sounds like a very convenient mode of worship and study, and it has even allowed the church to fulfill its noble challenge of getting the Gospel into all parts of the earth, this social media phenomenon for many has been nothing short of a miracle, because of this, I believe we should consider the pros and cons of social media on Sunday Morning.

Pros of Social Media On Sunday Mornings

- Keeps members who can't attend connected.
- Encourages people in their own setting anytime of the day or night.
- Allows people to visit your ministry that otherwise may never come.
- Wonderful tool for reaching all generations particularly the millennials.
- A new formation of community and fellowship is taking place regarding the use of technology.
- In regards to income, many more people are able to participate and be a blessing to the ministry financially because they are connected.

Cons of Social Media on Sunday Mornings

- Members get lazy and decide to stay home and not attend. While on-line numbers may be high, it can kill local attendance of the church.

- Bad videos, misquoted tweets and summaries can often distort the message and compromise levels of excellence.

- While no worship is perfect, when errors and gaffs are made, it allows people who have no sense of church to chime in with their "two-cent worth," oftentimes leaving derogatory statements, bringing shame to the body of Christ.

- Over-exposure is a high risk. People get so accustomed to hearing and seeing the worship, that the mystery of the moment is removed, and worship is just another thing to do on social media.

- While many churches are being blessed by online giving, other churches may not have the loyalty factor in place, so that when members miss worship, the money is missing too.

- With everybody scrolling and fumbling with cell phones and iPads in worship, there are times when these things can be so distracting.

Let's Talk Sunday Morning- How Do We Handle Social Media In The Church?

Since social media is here, the church in some way must succumb to the forms of communication for which the world exists. It is incumbent of us to consider how we can make social media work for the church, and in turn, allow the church to take back Sunday Morning.

The Theology and Facebook

The Theology of Facebook deals with understanding Facebook for a God perspective. This is not to suggest that we know exactly what God is thinking, but looking at Facebook from a God perspective can help illuminate how face book can become a hindrance to our relationship with God if we are not careful.

Can I Be Your Friend?

The predominant feature of Facebook, is that it is a place where one can have presumed "friends." This "friend" idea is not by accident. Because if we were to relate the term "friend" to the inception of the website it would make sense. Mark Zuckerberg created Facebook at a time when he needed a friend. His girlfriend had just dumped him, and if there is anything he felt that could help him get over her, it would have been another friend. In other words, this social website was created out of a need for a friend. Thus today we have 400 million people who spend most of their day looking for "friends" for whom they can connect with and even develop some kind of relationship with.

The concern with looking for a friend on Facebook in someway reduces tremendously the value of a friend. There was a time when this word had great meaning and value, and was a label that was only applied in relationships that were proven and tested. "The language of friendship is not words but meanings." –Henry David Thoreau. Here is what I am after everybody is not qualified to be called your friend. A friend is someone who will be there for you when things are thick and thin. A friend will support you when others fail you. A friend will tell you the truth, even when it is not popular to do so. A friend will challenge you to be the best you, all the while not being envious or jealous when you become it. A friend will not judge you for where you are, but can always see what you have the potential of becoming.

Friends are very difficult to come by, however, Facebook has made the process very simple and easy. So easy until all you have to do is click a button. This may not be so much about Mark Zuckerberg's break up, but it might say something about our own breakup with ourselves. What does the need to having over 300 hundred friends on your site do for you, particularly when Proverbs 18:24 declares, "The man of many friends [a friend of all the world] will prove himself a bad friend, but there is a friend who sticks closer than a brother." "Bad friend" does not mean that you are a bad person, it just says that with the meaning of friend from a biblical perspective, involved much more than a click of the button. Friendship is about loyalty, sacrifice, accountability and respect. If all of your 300 friends on your site can prove themselves to you in this way, by all means call them your friend, but if by chance they cannot, are they really your friend. "Sometimes you put walls up not to keep people out, but to see who cares enough to break them down."

If you are in search for a friend, know that Christ is that friend. Lest I sound more heavenly bound than earthly good, the Spirit of Christ will lead you to friends by the Spirit. Yes, some great things happen via technology, more specifically Facebook, but even there, allow the Spirit of God to lead you and help you to discern who is the right friend for you.

Please Accept Me?

Another feature that is predominant on Facebook is the way the system is set up. Once you recognize a face that you know or that you would like to know, the system will take you through a process where you must ask the person if they will accept you as their friend. If they accept you then you have access to their entire Facebook world. Hooray!

Perhaps the genesis of this "acceptance" thing came during the time when Mark Zuckerburg-founder of Facebook was feeling like his girlfriend didn't accept him. His history records that she dumped him. For people who feel like they have been dumped all of their lives, never able to be successful in a relationship, never fully appreciated and confirmed by anyone, those words "accepted" must have tremendous value when you finally score with a "friend" you may not even know. To be accepted is a great thing, but we must keep in context whom you are being accepted by.

Some of those we are accepting on Facebook are people that perhaps we don't need to accept. Because the way the system works is that a person that you have been delivered from for 10 years can by chance see you on Facebook, and simply request to be your friend. You accept them, and from there the communication starts all over again. At the time, it seems like a simple gesture of communication, but from the plateau of the spiritual, it can also be a way that the enemy is trying to introduce you to someone that God has already delivered you from. Not in all cases, but perhaps in some. Before you know it, a Facebook conversation ends up with face to face interaction, and for 10 years you have been free of drama, cheating, fussing and fighting, and all because of a simple "click" and an "acceptance" you are in that vicious cycle again.

So the critical thing is not to allow your need for acceptance to get you into a position of allowing spirits in your life that are there to uphold you where God presently has you. You have been delivered and already on another highway. Stay there. You are accepted when you make Christ your Savior, and when Christ accepts you, know who you are, apart from Facebook. You are the Lord's child, and you are wonderfully made in the image of God; and know that God alone accepts you even when others do not.

Picture This

What really makes Facebook a drawing place for millions of fabulous and sometimes bizarre pictures and personal information that you are able to explore. While it is always nice to show the world how beautiful and handsome you are, there have been many people who have gotten in trouble because of pictures and personal information posted on their Facebook page.

Many workplaces, universities, and other agencies are now using Facebook to get a sense of your character, interactions, and the company you keep. Since this is happening, the questions that we must explore are: what is appropriate for a Christian's Facebook page, how much should be revealed, what are the venues where this information can be circulated, and how do you safeguard yourself from any fraud practice? These are just a few questions that need to be considered, therefore consider the observations below as a guide for having a Facebook relationship.

Facebook and The Church

- Facebook for a Christian should not contain any information that reveals their personal address, work location, daily routine, schedule, family dialogue, or personal conflicts that you recently had.

- Facebook for a Christian should not bear pictures that do not represent Christ and the Kingdom. It should not reflect exposed sensual body shots, social pictures that may be perceived as you drinking or smoking, performing sexual acts or, compromising positions.

- Facebook for a Christian should not be a site that fosters gossip where the conversation cannot be verified about the other for who is being discussed. Personal insults and attacks should not be found on this site.

- Facebook for a Christian should represent good character and a page that would reflect the high standards that you possess as a Christian. Therefore, you must even be cautious who you accept as a friend because their picture and information will eventfully be a representation for you.

The Theology of the Blog

In the book of Genesis it is evident that Adam and Eve had been the victims of a blog- or information proven not to be true. Satan blogged Adam and Eve and told them that what God spoke of the tree of knowledge was not necessarily true. Satan made them believe that they could eat from the tree, and no harm would come upon them. Adam and Eve did eat, and sin became human kinds ultimate fate. However, in my analysis of this story, the sin is not so much that they ate, the sin is they believed what was told to them by the serpent, and they put more confidence in what the serpent said, trusting over what he said, rather than trusting what God said. And just like a good blogger, Satan plants the seed, and then slowly goes behind the curtain, and leaves the drama between Adam, Eve, and humanity with a cameo performance on the stage.

This notion of blogging and a rumor being spread about you unjustifiably takes grace and mercy to a another level. Since it is so easy for someone to blog and plant seeds of suspicion in churches, marriages, dating relationships, friendships, and even business acquaintances, every day you live and your name has not been blogged you should thank God for grace and mercy. With blogging being so easy to do, the favor on your life is even threatened. Because Proverbs 22:1 says, "A good name is rather to be chosen than great riches, and loving favor rather than silver and gold." The writer indicates that favor is attached to a good name. Therefore, if someone blogs against your good name, unjustifiably, might I add, and then there is some favor in the eyes of people that is sure to shift. This is because it is human nature people to believe some things even if it proves not to be true. Therefore, you must understand your value and yourself especially when you are the victim of a blog. Do those people who are blogging you really know you? Do they have any knowledge about the destiny God has prepared for your life? Do these strangers even have a clue about what God has whispered in your ear, and about what He is ready to do with your life? You are blessed and destined for promotion, now let them go and blog that!

Blogging and the Church

- Christians should never blog any information that is going to be damaging to the kingdom of God. Remember every time you blog a Christian in bad light, you are also blogging the name of Christ.

- If you have ever put any false information about someone on any blogging website, you owe it to the individual to go back, correct it, or make it right.

- Whatever information is blogged, make certain that it can be proven and that it is indeed factual. A good rule of thumb is if someone pursues to find out who it is that is posting, can you be sued for slander.

- When you are blogging, always remember what you are blogging about, particularly if it is a person's character that is being addressed, know that you are actually talking about a person that has a family, that may have children, and more importantly, they may be a Christian. The fundamental question that you should raise is, would I want this said about me, if the tables were turned.

The Theology of Tweeting

There is a very popular phenomenon that is sweeping the globe called "tweeting". Twitter is a social networking micro-blogging service that was created by Jack Dorsey in 2006. Tweets are text based that can be posted on an authors page and the words are delivered to the followers of the author. In other words, if a person wants to know what the day is like for a celebrity, the celebrity can "tweet" or "text" their activity of their day, and the people that are following the celebrity feel connected to the celebrity and in some way, enter into their intimate personal lives. For example, celebrities are tweeting when they brush their teeth, how they are wearing their hair that day, what they are eating for dinner, and what movie they are working on or song they're recording. It is possible that a celebrity would have hundreds and thousands of followers.

My advice to you who enjoy tweeting is to keep it in perspective. Know that when someone is communicating to you on a mass level, you are a part of a mass following. I would also like to mention that these kinds of social networking tools can be addictive. Monitor how much time you spend doing this a day, and try to occupy your time with something that will be more meaningful for you in the future. If you are tweeting, be mindful of the personal information that you share. I had a friend that tweeted all of her followers and said," I am going out of town for the next few days, so everyone pray for me while I get some rest". Wow, this was good news for a criminal or a thief.

Tweeting and the Church

However the theology of tweeting takes root in us, understand how through the Word of God, God has already tweeted us, there are intimate details about God's nature and character that we can view. If God has tweeted us through His Word, then all God is looking for are followers. Are you a follower of Christ? If you are, then my word to you is spend more time tweeting with God, tune into what God is desiring and what God is doing so that you can more passionately follow Him.

Always remember that what we are seeking from others and expecting from others, God is expecting from us. [9] The LORD also will be a refuge for the oppressed, a refuge in times of trouble. [10] And they that know thy name will put their trust in thee: for thou, LORD, hast not forsaken them that seek thee. While social networking can be very positive, I believe that God is more interested in us networking with Him and the things that God is connected to in the Kingdom. If social networking for you is a result of some void feeling in your life, know that God is able to fulfill your void through His Word, and Christ is a friend that sticks closer than a brother. Network with Him, and you will be fine!

Let's Talk Sunday Morning and Social Media

- Social media should be used for marketing, educating, and inspiration. Sharing positive stories and church news is a real winner for social media.

- Every church needs to consider its role with social media, and how that particular church chooses to engage.

- The use of social media should be well instructed, and even take a moment and let the congregation know that it is is to reach beyond the congregation, and not "shrink" the congregation.

- Social media should assist the church in its mission and not become a detractor, deterant, or a distraction. In worship, don't miss a moment trying to catch a note.

- Social media might be good for worship, study, and even some forms of evangelism, but social media can never replace biblical 'koinonia' (fellowship) with the kingdom of God.

Sunday Morning Group Discussion Questions

1. Do you think social media has helped or hurt the Sunday Morning worship?

_____

_____

_____

2. What is the preferred social media sight for you, and how do you use it for the Kingdom?

_____

_____

_____

3. How do you help defend the church on social media, and can you recall a time when that happened?

_____

_____

_____

4. What are some ways you use social media to promote the Kingdom?

_____

_____

_____

Sign up to post

What The Church Must Do To Get People Back In Church

Since reading this material, it would be necessary to provide some very practical methodologies for churches to use in their approach of getting people back in church. While every church must do an assessment on what works best in their own setting, Rainer does provide some approaches that are practical, doable, meaningful, and I believe can work if supported by dedication and determination. Consider these moves we must make to take back Sunday Morning.

We must realize that Christianity is not what it used to be. We must accept the reality that Christianity as we knew it in the past is gone, or at best very rare to find. The Coronavirus and the concept of "Social Distancing", has given the church a new face. The church that was there when our parents took us to church is gone, and we must accept that as a reality. The church that was there when our parents took us to church is gone, and we must accept that as a reality. Therefore, instead of trying to revive the past, let's put our energy in fueling the future. Never forget that the windshield is always larger than the rearview mirror. Meaning, our ministry approach should be much like that African Sankofa bird that has the ability to fly forward while looking backwards. Honor our past, but move forward with the future.

We must realize that if God changes, the Church must change too.

God's substance will never change, but how God manifests Himself does change. In other words, in the Old Testament God shows up as fire, a still small voice, and earthquakes. In the New Testament He shows up in the flesh as Christ. In the book of Acts, God is present by way of Holy Spirit. His substance never changes, but how He manifests Himself does change. Essentially, if God changes methods, the Church should too. Pray against being a stuck church, and fight against the temptation of saying, "We have never done it this way before," "It doesn't take all of that," and " Why change now."

We must realize that the Church is not a museum, but it is more of a hotel. In a museum people come to see artifacts of value, often with the mindset that you do not touch what you see. There is a feeling of boundaries established that you cannot cross. However, whenever one checks into a hotel, the intent, most of the time, is to rest, have a place to relieve burden, realizing that the stay won't be too long. This is indicative of the church. We must be more like a hotel, a place of rest, existing to dispatch disciples to their next destination or assignment. Therefore, hospitality is critical, treating people with respect and honor is crucial, and serving is top priority. Tom Rainer put it this way, "Your church is not a country club where you pay dues to get your perks and privileges. It is a Gospel outpost where you are to put yourself last. Don't seek to get your way with the music, temperature, and length of sermons. Here is a simple guideline: Be willing to die for the sake of the Gospel."

We must stop fighting among ourselves. The Church is the only place I know where the team fights against itself. We must get rid of the mentality that if I can't have it my way, or if I don't like the way things are going, then I will sink this ship. Never forget that the Church is the bride of Christ, and it is impossible to love Christ, and abuse His wife. If there are things about the church you are not happy with, pray about it, but do not post it on social media, talk about your issues in barber shops and beauty parlors, or start movements publicly to prove your point. Pray and be the Church.

We must explain our language. Much of our language the church doesn't understand, therefore, you know the unchurched does not understand. If you use words that are popular among the church like "saved", "sanctified", "repentance", and "contrition", be ready to explain what these words mean. Break it down, and always be ready to explain your faith at a 3rd grade level of learning. You will win every time. Even the most unintelligent person in your congregation passed the 3rd grade.

We must focus on the majors and not the minors. I have learned that if the matter does not threaten the core existence of the Church, then everything else is minor. The Church needs leaders that are solution oriented, rather than problem seekers. Keep the main thing, the main thing; worship, study, fellowship, evangelism, prayer, giving, and love.

We must make prayer a priority for our churches. It is really this simple, the Church must return back to prayer. Little prayer, little power. Much prayer, much power. It's just that simple.

WHAT'S NEXT?
REDEEMING SUNDAY AND
RENEWING CHURCHES

Bill J. Leonard, P.hD.

*I*n this important study, Bishop Sir Walter Mack calls Christians to respond to the challenges confronting churches in 21st century America. He describes those challenges as they impact congregations throughout the country, with particular implications for the Church's traditional approaches to Sunday worship. The book is a call to action for congregations representing a broad denominational, theological and racial spectrum. It is a recognition that American Christianity is experiencing major changes impacted by transitions in American society at large. These trends include the following:

> *Denominational systems are disconnecting, disengaging, and debating; many are fragmenting organizationally.*

> *Fewer individuals think of their primary Christian identity as a denominational identity.*

> *Many denominationally oriented congregations now minimize relationships with parent bodies.*

> *By many estimates at least 4,000 churches close their doors or merge annually.*

> *Multiple studies indicate that one in five Americans now claim no religious affiliation. These so-called "nones" now represent the largest single religious designation in the U.S. (One in three Americans ages 18-30 identify themselves as "nones.") These numbers appear to increase annually.*

> *Many of the religiously non-affiliated refer to themselves as "believers, not belongers" or "spiritual but not religious," often pursuing personal spirituality but outside the confines of traditional or sectarian religion.*

> *Numerical declines have long been present among the so-called Mainline denominations (The Episcopal Church, the Presbyterian Church USA, the United Methodist Church, the United Church of Christ, the American Baptist Churches USA, the Disciples of Christ, The Moravian Church). These groups currently represent some 13% of Americans.*

- *The 21st century brought declines or at least membership slowdowns to a variety of groups labeled evangelical. These include the Presbyterian Church in America, the Southern Baptist Convention, a variety of other Baptist groups including Independent, Primitive, Free Will Baptists, as well as certain predominately African American denominations such as the National Baptist Convention USA, the National Baptist Convention of America, and the Progressive National Baptist Convention. Pentecostal-oriented denominations such as the Assemblies of God, the Church of God-Cleveland, Tennessee, and the United Pentecostal Church, while more statistically stable, also show early signs of decline. These groups represent some 20% of Americans.*

> *Indications are that in 21st century America, 80% of senior adults are white and Christian, while only 29% of young adults are white and Christian.*

> *As fewer families attend church regularly, if at all, congregations enlist fewer children and youth to be nurtured to faith.*

> *As fewer adults attend church, fewer adults claim to experience Christian conversion.*

> *Declining attendance impacts membership and baptisms as well as Sunday Schools (a traditional source of Christian nurture and instruction), church finances, upkeep on church buildings, and the shaping of Christian community.*

> *Declining or inconsistent Sunday attendance means that fewer people, even church members, study the Bible consistently through Sunday School or in hearing the preached Word. Basic biblical knowledge or references cannot be taken for granted, even among those connected to churches.*

> *As this book documents, these changes both impact and are impacted by the changing sociology of Sunday.*

The term "the changing sociology of Sunday," means that throughout American society Sunday has become a day for responding to a variety of familial, recreational, travel, and job-related opportunities and demands. One important symbol of that changing sociology can be summed up in a single word: soccer. Those Sunday practice are well known to families across the country as families adjust their church attendance to the schedules of Sunday soccer or other sporting events involving children and grandchildren. Soccer is only one illustration of changes in the rhythm and rituals of Sunday impacting those engaged with and disengaged from church activities. For many church members, Sunday attendance may be problematic, less because they are choosing not to participate, than the reality of additional demands made upon them in ways that limit Sunday church attendance.

As this book indicates, congregations must give serious attention to these changing dynamics and their impact on faith communities. Failure to take these social transitions seriously or develop strategies for responding to spiritual and demographic declines already creates serious difficulties for many congregations, and often contributes to church closings. By ignoring these realities, churches complicate their organizational life and their future. It is imperative that faith communities develop strategies for responding to these transitions in religious and cultural life.

Many congregations are responding to these challenges. The following is a representative but not definitive survey of options that are available.

Congregations: Strategies for the Future

> **Congregations must be clear about their own identity—who they are, what they believe, and how they seek to minister inside and outside the church.**

In an earlier era, denominations played an important role in shaping congregational identity. Denominations facilitated publications, education, and mission, as well as a sense of history and tradition, nurtured and passed on from generation to generation. While denominational identity still has its place in some congregations, others find it increasingly less viable. There is considerable indication that many families, when moving from one place to another, are apt to look for a congregation that feels spiritually, doctrinally or communally like the church they departed, before they look at its denominational designation.

> **Congregational Identity:**
A Hospitable Traditionalism

As congregations describe and enact their identity, they begin with a specific traditionalism, the ways in which they identify with a specific Christian tradition; the meaning of baptism, the Lord's Supper and other rituals that identify their practice of Christianity; their understanding of the nature of salvation, entering into faith and going on in grace.

In the 21st century, congregations cannot take it for granted that those who attend understand that identity, so it is very important that they are clear about those issues. These traditions are shaped by scripture and history, by denominational and ecumenical relationships, and by the way in which congregations carry out their mission in the world. At the same time, traditionalism must not turn a faith community inward on itself but outward on the world. Churches are called to be hospitable, welcoming the stranger, open to saint and sinner alike, calling persons to faith and new life in Christ. Instructing members old and new in the meaning of that hospitable traditionalism is an essential calling of every congregation.

> **In confronting cultural transitions and social needs, congregations would do well to begin by asking, "Is our church thriving?" before asking, "Is our church growing numerically?"**

A "thriving" congregation is one that energizes its members to engage in specific ministries inside and particularly outside the church. Again, congregations need to be intentional about responding to specific needs around them. The era of anticipating that potential members will simply show up at the church door is essentially over. Now more than ever churches must provide ministry to persons outside the faith community. Congregations begin by surveying the needs around them and then deciding how to respond to those needs. Some churches are large enough to develop multiple ministries, while other smaller congregations may only be able to focus on a few of those community needs. The number of specific ministries is perhaps less significant than the ability of churches to energize members in participating in ministry and mission.

> **In light of the changing sociology of Sunday, many congregations are revisiting options for providing multiple occasions for worship.**

Options for worship are nothing new, but the changing sociology of Sunday has made those options even more important for congregational ministry. Some churches of course, offer multiple Sunday services as options for addressing individual's schedules. It is also important to acknowledge that the eleven o'clock traditional worship hour was in many ways the result of a much earlier era informed by a more rural culture that required early morning chores and time to get from home to church. Later congregations scheduled Sunday School as the first Sunday event, followed by morning worship. Much of that is changed in the 21st century.

Options include:

- Multiple Sunday services, some of which are intentionally shortened to fit diverse schedules.

- Multiple options for gathering throughout the week: Bible studies and church suppers mid-week; early evening services available for members on their way home from work; noon-time services aimed at the lunch hour, often with meals provided.

- Offering occasions when persons can receive Holy Communion throughout the week.

- Responding to the decline in Sunday School, some congregations offer additional small group experiences for Bible and other instruction in homes, restaurants, gyms, and other locales throughout the week.

> **Congregations are developing signature ministries that make meaningful contributions to their communities.**

Many 21st century congregations that seem to be "thriving" are those that have cultivated signature ministries in their communities, response to pressing needs in their local settings. No doubt congregations have long shared those ministries in their communities, but many are realizing in new ways that their own survival depends on going to the people with the Gospel rather than anticipating that people will come to them in traditional ways.

These signature ministries can be long term or short term, involving elaborate or limited programs. Some have involved diverse types of worship services, music programs or teaching forums. Other programs involve traditional ministries that provide clothing, food and financial assistance to individuals in need. Still others include tutorials for students; liturgical dance training for males and females; community engagement ministries may also involve divorce recovery workshops, drug and alcohol abuse groups, voter registration, hospice ministry, and day care for target groups from children to senior adults. Whatever the options, these ministries are specifically focused on providing ministry in the larger community, sometimes facilitated by one congregation, sometimes offered through a coalition of faith communities.

> **Congregations might renew a commitment to the Jesus story and the retelling of that story in 21st century American culture.**

The Jesus story is the heart of the Christian Gospel. It forms the Church's message, its identity, and its mission in the world. Across the centuries Christians have found innumerable ways to tell and retell the Jesus story. Learning and relearning the story and its meaning is a continuing call and challenge for Christ's church. It appears that many 21st century Americans are choosing to distance themselves, if not from the Jesus Story, then perhaps the Church's way of telling that story. If that is the case, then how might churches recover and retell that ancient story in ways that capture the attention and perhaps the hearts of persons living in these times?

At the beginning of the 20th century, missionary-musician-physician, Albert Schweitzer, called the church of his day to rediscover the Jesus story for their times. His classic book, *The Quest of the Historical Jesus,* published in 1906, contains this challenge, a challenge worth considering over a century later:

He comes to us as One unknown, without a name, as of old, by the lakeside, He came to those... who knew Him not. He speaks to us the same words: "Follow thou me!" and sets us to the tasks which He has to fulfill for our time. He commands. And to those who obey Him, whether they be wise or simple, He will reveal Himself in the toils, the conflicts, the sufferings which they shall pass through in His fellowship, and, as an inexplicable mystery, they shall learn in their own experience Who He is."

May God grant us the courage to reclaim that calling and carry it with us into the world.

BOOK ENDORSEMENT

As Pastors struggle with the decline in church attendance, Bishop Sir Walter Mack has written a concise and yet insightful book that addresses the reasons why people are not as inclined to attend church as they once were. Written for clergy and laypersons, this book reveals the ways that the world and the church itself contribute to the decline and practical ways we can reverse the trend. This book is a must read for those who seek to restore the body of Christ to its rightful place in the lives of believers and the world.

–Cynthia L. Hale, Senior Pastor
Ray of Hope Christian Church,
Decatur, Georgia

In this book, Bishop Sir Walter Lee Mack, Jr., with passion, purpose, as well as scholarly research, and keen discernment and insight, addresses the dilemma and reality of the dethroning of Sunday Morning as the fulcrum for Christian nurture and Kingdom witness and expansion. How does Sunday Morning regain its savor for both the majority of individuals who should be filling the pews, but are presently filling shopping malls and the bleachers at sporting events?

–William D. Watley
St. Phillip A.M.E. Church
Atlanta, Georgia

In this important study, Bishop Sir Walter Mack calls Christians to respond to the challenges confronting churches in 21st century America. He describes those challenges as they impact congregations throughout the country, with particular implications for the Church's traditional approaches to Sunday worship. The book is a call to action for congregations representing a broad denominational, theological and racial spectrum. It is a recognition that American Christianity is experiencing major changes impacted by transitions in American society at large.

–Bill J. Leonard
Wake Forest University Divinity School
Former Dean